# A PASSION FOR JUSTICE
## THE STORIES OF JOE KENYON

# A PASSION FOR JUSTICE
## THE STORIES OF JOE KENYON

## JOE KENYON

Edited by David Donnison

TRENT EDITIONS

Published by Trent Editions   2003

Trent Editions
Department of English and Media Studies
The Nottingham Trent University
Clifton Lane.
Nottingham NG11 8NS

Printed in Great Britain by Goaters Limited, Nottingham

ISBN 1 84233 082 9

# Contents

## III Roving Radical

# *Introduction*

When I took the chair of the Supplementary Benefits Commission in 1975 I was looking for people who would speak effectively for those who depended on the social assistance payments we were responsible for – roughly speaking, the payments now described as income support and job seekers' allowance. That search soon led me to Joe Kenyon. Living on supplementary benefit himself, he was an expert on every aspect of the system, a resolute and effective champion for those who depended on it, and a vivid, loveable man. I had to answer many letters from Joe, writing on behalf of his clients in the years that followed, and we met from time to time.

When I returned to University work in 1980 Joe was one of the friends made during my time at the Commission whom I kept in touch with. Sixteen years later his beloved wife Irene died after a long and painful illness. Utterly exhausted by grief and the stress of nursing her, Joe too seemed likely to die. He certainly wanted to. Then he began writing the stories he had told Irene during her sleepless nights of pain, and they renewed his will to live. From time to time he sent batches of them to me and a few other friends. I offered some advice, but my main plea to him was to keep going and write more. They were such a powerful account of a world now disappearing from living memory, bearing so many messages that should be handed on to future generations.

In 1998 I took Joe to the annual conference of the Social Policy Association, full of teachers and researchers working in that field, and invited him to tell us some of his stories as an after-dinner speech. Although he said shyly that he had never made such a speech and did not know whether anyone would be interested, he took complete command of his audience, told several stories in his gently mischievous Yorkshire style, and was kept up till the small hours by my younger colleagues who plied him with pints and asked for more. It was a heart-warming and greatly encouraging evening for him. Encouraging, too, were requests for his stories from the *London Review of Books, The Sunday Telegraph* and the BBC's Yorkshire radio station – for whom he spoke fluently, without a single note.

As more and more stories reached me, I was soon pleading with Joe to gather them into a book; then, if he wished, write some more for a second volume. But it dawned on me that, increasingly ill as he was, it was his continuing determination to write another story that was keeping him going. That, and the battles he was still fighting with officials, social workers, doctors and nurses – increasingly his own carers – whenever he felt they were failing in their duty. Clearly he was never going to finish the book. Early in 2000, when I visited him in a Sheffield hospital, he was plainly dying, tended by nurses who had fallen in love with him, and still talking about his next story and the Social Policy Conference in July to which he wanted to go. Then, two or three weeks later, his son Frank telephoned to say that his Dad had asked me to edit and publish the book. Joe died a few days later.

Hammered out on an old manual typewriter when he was ill and often in pain, the stories were pure, if somewhat encrusted, gold. With help from Frank, Joe's sister, May Wray and her husband, Bernard, who worked in the pit with him, I have tried to clean off the encrustations, shake the tales out into a helpful order, and let their quality shine through in Joe's own words. A few footnotes at the end of the book provide clarifications, explaining terms or adding brief incidents and explanations told to me by Joe or his family. I also changed the book title (Joe once suggested the title 'Just Me'), gave titles to its three parts, and made a few changes to the names of stories. Readers who would like to study the original typescript will find it in the Library of the Northern College where it has been catalogued with his books, journals and files.

Joe tells us about his life in the pages that follow, but a brief outline of it may help readers to appreciate the significance of these stories. He was born in Carlton village, near Barnsley in Yorkshire, in 1915 – the third of seven surviving children. (There were two more who died soon after they were born.) His family were compelled, soon after the first world war, to live on the pittance provided by public assistance. His father, who had been a miner in the pits around Barnsley, was unable to perform heavy work because he had tuberculosis, which had been complicated by exposure to gas during the war. By arguing that his illness was due to causes other than his employment the colliery escaped any responsibility for compensating him. All Joe's father could manage, when well enough, were night watchman duties for a while, and sometimes working for the Council shifting snow.

With their father frequently confined in distant sanitoria, life was very hard for the Kenyons. The children were often unable to go to school because their mother could not provide shoes and clothing for them, and Joe was largely self-educated. He got a job in a local pit at the age of fourteen and continued to read voraciously – about economics, politics, logic, law, health and safety regulations, mining technology, and much else. The sixpence his mother returned to him when he handed her his first week's wages was spent on a second-hand dictionary. Although he tried other jobs from time to time – some of them vividly described in these stores – he always returned to Barnsley and the pits until the Second World War took him into the forces.

It was during a week-end's leave that Joe met Irene, with whom he had a love affair that continued till her death, more than fifty years later. At first they could not marry, since Irene's husband had gone missing, presumed dead, in France. It was only when his death was confirmed that they were able to get married.

Joe returned to the pits after the war and became increasingly involved in trade union work, refusing opportunities for promotion into management, acceptance of which he felt would have been a betrayal of his comrades.

When the dust finally caught up with Joe in 1960, compelling him to leave colliery work, he became an organiser and teacher for the National Council of Labour Colleges, which offered a radical education for working class people. That was in many ways an ideal job for this intelligent, widely-read and aggressively independent man – until the Trade Unions took over the NCLC and insisted that its teachers produce well-trained union officials, not revolutionaries.

Joe then joined Equity, the actors' union, as one of their local officials. In time he had difficulties in accepting practices which he felt were not in the interests of their members – mainly youngsters playing in the clubs around Yorkshire. He moved on again to become a welfare rights specialist in one of the Community Development Projects set up by the Home Office.

Thereafter he became an unpaid but very active welfare rights advocate and advisor, calling himself the National Unemployed Workers' Union. He was very effective at this, and press reports and television appearances gave him a nationwide reputation. People wrote from all over the country to seek his help – sometimes with no more than 'Joe Kenyon, Barnsley' on the envelope.

Irene, who had been a constant supporter for Joe and their two sons, became ill with cancer in the mid-1990s. It was then that Joe started telling these tales to her when she was unable to sleep for pain. He added some more after her death, but the loving, fearful, pain-filled darkness in which most of these memories were recovered is the setting readers need to bear in mind as they explore this book. Spoken in Joe's gentle Barnsley accent, these tales come out of a Yorkshire working-class oral tradition – to be heard rather than read. Written in no particular order, they are full of gaps, omitting important things like the birth and upbringing of their sons, that Irene would not have needed to be told about.

So *A Passion for Justice* is not Joe Kenyon's autobiography. It doesn't tell about his two sons, Alf born in 1941 and Frank born in 1943; nor the homes he and Irene lived in till they came to rest in a council house on the edge of Barnsley in the early 1960s; nor about his brothers and sisters; nor his mother, who lived to the age of 73. It doesn't tell about Irene's early life and work – at first on a farm, then in a hotel in Leeds, then in a tank factory during the war, and later, when the boys were about ten, back to factories of every kind and work in a market garden. It doesn't tell about Joe's swimming pranks: how he would go out to the canal bridge where there was always a crowd on a sunny Saturday, walk precariously along its parapet and then, to everyone's consternation, 'accidentally' fall in. Swimming beneath the water under the bridge, he would climb out on the far side where his sister, May, had hidden a bag of clothes for him behind a tree. Having got dressed, he would walk round and saunter through the crowd – by now shouting that he must have drowned – and ask them what was happening.

It doesn't tell about Joe's wartime experiences, some of which were gently delinquent, as when his time spent guarding military stores enabled him to pass out a few useful things – cigarettes, a greatcoat – to the officers and so get 48-hour passes to visit Irene. Nor does it tell about how Joe's work in the turbulent Batley Community Development Project was so successful in getting people their rights from the social security and local authority services that the Council eventually got rid of him.

Nor does it tell of the full extent of Joe's many years of unpaid welfare rights work which brought appeals for help from all over the country: how he would drive, while he still had an old banger, and later just hitch-hike and bus his way to interview people having a hard time and do his best to get them some justice by advising them, writing letters for them, and representing them at tribunals.

Instead of an autobiography, *A Passion for Justice* is simply the memories Joe would talk about with Irene during the night hours when, at the end of her life, in pain and unable to sleep, she would turn to him and say, "Tell me a story Joe" – plus a few other experiences and thoughts he wanted to leave behind him.

Full of moral meanings and implications for action, these stories lead towards the concluding chapter Joe was never able to write. I cannot write it for him, but he challenges each of us to reflect on the conclusions we would draw for ourselves. I offer mine in the Postscript at the end of this book.

David Donnison

## DEDICATION

This book is dedicated to my dearly beloved wife Irene who, for nigh on fifty years, loved, cared for me, and gave me so much happiness and joy. During the last year of her life, when she was often in pain and unable to sleep, she would move closer to me, rest her head on my breast and say, "Tell me a story love." These were the stories I told her. Now my only prayer is that somehow, some day, I can embrace her once again and tell her another story.

Joe Kenyon

# I GROWING UP

## LIFE IN THE BALANCE

I was born on the 27th of July 1915. For two years my life was in the balance. I was tormented by boils which covered my whole body – two hundred at a time, they told me later. My arms, legs, feet, indeed every part of me, were so sensitive to even the slightest touch, I had at all times to be held on a pillow, nursed on a pillow, carried on a pillow, and put to sleep on a pillow, under almost constant surveillance. It was impossible for me to be picked up, nursed, or hugged and kissed like any other baby. Any attempt to do so was too painful and distressing for me, and, I'm sure, for my parents.

What agonies of worry and despair my Mum and Dad must have endured I have no way of telling. I only know from my own experience how worried I have been when my children were 'only' a bit off colour. Mrs Nicholson, our God-given neighbour, helped untiringly to look over me, to wash and clean me, and to comfort Mum and Dad. Indeed, she became so fond of me, she in later years favoured me as one of her own. She would often say "For two years you struggled and fought to live, and now look at you." In return, I have often thought "If I can survive that, I can survive anything."

Naturally, I cannot recall any of this. I was too young for the memory of it to be registered in my conscious mind. But I have often wondered, can it be locked in my subconscious mind – recorded somewhere within my inner self? Does it affect my thinking, my beliefs and concerns? The fight to live, to hold on to life, the agonies that Mum and Dad must have endured, the pain that the tiny body must have fought; locked within my psyche, but not remembered; do they explain how, even as a child, I used to worry for other people? I only know that, throughout my life, I have always felt a close affinity with other people; always cared for others in pain or misfortune, ready to take on a fight for anyone I thought had been mistreated.

Whenever the Annual Fair visited the village, I would walk around the fairground and watch the carousel, the roundabouts, or dobby horses as we used to call them. If there were only a few people riding, I would worry for the fairground man; would wish that more people would ride, so that he would earn a good living – even though my own family was in poverty and I never had a single penny to buy a ride for myself. The only ride I ever got was when I used to leap on to the step, cling to the highly polished brass upright and ride around, once, twice and sometimes three times, before I was hauled off by an irate attendant. It's the way I've been all my life. And my wife loved me for it. Rebellious, but caring for people.

I was approaching my second birthday when a new doctor came into the village. Dr Eskridge was a big burly man, rough and down to earth in his speech, always dressed in tweed plus-fours and smoking a big cigar. He was very much concerned for me and for several weeks visited me every day. Then he decided to vaccinate me, four times on my left arm and shoulder. The vaccinations left four great big scars which I carried with me well into my thirties. From the day I was vaccinated, I began to recover from my sickness, the boils disappeared and I began to thrive. By the time I was three, I had learned to walk and talk, and even though I was getting much better in health, old Eskridge visited me twice a week for a very long time. For frequent periods of my third year, I was confined to bed. The bed was kept downstairs, in the living room, so that I was always under observation. My Dad hung his Army steel mirror by a long string, attached to the ceiling. It was hung at a height where I could easily strike it, making a wonderful mellow clang that vibrated for a few seconds after. My memory of that time is as fresh now as if it was only yesterday. By the time I was five, although small, I was as robust and healthy as the rest of my mates. I was able to start school and take part in all the games. It was a large school divided into two sections; one for the boys and one for the girls. We even had separate playgrounds and woe betide anyone who trespassed into the wrong one.

At this time, we weren't too bad off. My Dad was at home and working – of all places down the pit. He was often ill, suffering from tuberculosis, and after a couple of years he was back in the sanatorium. Sometimes he was at Ilkley; at other times he was at Maidstone in Kent. It wasn't so bad for Mum when he was at Ilkley because she was able to visit him once every month. But when he was at Maidstone visits were out of the question. Mum always wrote to Dad every Thursday. Thursday was the day when the food voucher came from the Parish. On his second spell in Maidstone I was about eight years old. Young Jimmy, my brother, was a baby, so I used to do most of the shopping. Stamped across the food voucher was a warning: 'Not to be used for the purchase of alcohol or tobacco'. But, in spite of that, the shopkeeper always let me have two packets of five Woodbine cigarettes: two pence a packet.

We were always more than ready for food when the voucher came. So after the shopping we would all have a bite to eat. Then my Mum would sit at the table to write her letter to Dad. At the end of the letter I would always add a few words as well. Mum would then put a silver sixpence in one of the cig packets, wrap the letter around the packets and put them in the envelope. Then with a kiss she would seal the envelope, and around the V shape of the gummed part at the back of the envelope she would print S.W.A.L.K. "Sealed With A Loving Kiss". I would then run up to the post office, buy a penny stamp, stick it on the envelope, give it a good kiss and drop it in the letter box.

It was hard going those days. The food voucher was only for seven shillings a week. Seven bob a week to buy food, clothes and anything else a family of five might need. Just a bob a day to keep five of us, a fraction more than tuppence a day for each of us: sheer bloody grinding poverty. The rent was four shillings and sixpence a week. The Guardians wouldn't allow anything for that because my Mum was paid five shillings a week from the pit benevolent fund.

Every Monday afternoon I walked the two and a half miles into the next village to collect the five bob from my Uncle Jack's house. He was the Secretary of the pit union. Monday was pay day for sick and disabled miners unable to work. It was always a pleasure to go to my Uncle Jack's. His wife, Aunt Helen, always made me very welcome, fussing around me. She wanted a son, but finished up with seven daughters trying for one. She always made sure I had a good lunch before I left for home.

It was probably my memories of the Benevolent Fund that prompted me to agitate for our own benevolent fund at North Gawber pit where I worked many years after. I was on the Branch Committee at the time. The fund was used to help the long-term sick, to pay for independent medical examinations for members who were appealing against decisions of the National Insurance Officers, and to pay the expenses of visits to sick members in the special chest hospitals at Barnsley and Wath Wood. Most of these men were dying of pneumoconiosis or other serious chest diseases. We used to take them money, gifts, and spend the afternoon with them. When they did finally leave the hospital most were carried away in a pine box.

At home, there was hardly enough food for us all. Except for bread. We always had plenty of good, home-baked bread. 'The staff of life' it was said. Plenty of bread, but often nowt to put on it: a sprinkling of sugar perhaps; or nothing if it was fresh out of the oven because that was best of all. Sometimes we had a bit of jam or dripping, and sometimes lard would do. Dinners, when we had one, were mostly potatoes mashed with swede, cabbage, Oxo and sometimes a bit of corned beef. As a treat, Mum would make a corned beef hash with lots of veg. Don't know how she managed it but it was always delicious. For Sunday she would buy six penn'orth of pie bits from the butcher, and would conjure up a good dinner. She was a great cook when she had the chance. When the belly is full, it makes for a certain feeling of well-being.

Mum learned her cooking while working in service during her teens. At that time there were very few job opportunities for girls within a mining community, and many of them went into service as maids for the wealthy middle class in the surrounding towns. Bradford, Batley and Dewsbury were places where many of the girls went. They were mill towns and provided plenty of mill work for the girls from pit villages like ours.

To get the family out of grinding poverty, my Mum decided to take in washing. One of the shops nearby was a newsagent and small grocery shop. They also made their own ice cream, which was famous for its quality. They were a family of seven. Two of their daughters were sent out selling ice cream in beautifully decorated carts, pulled by a pony. The three other children were of school age. It was my job, along with my sister Selina, to go along to the shop on a Sunday evening and collect a large basket of family washing, and a number of white coats which the ice cream sellers wore.

Monday morning, Mum was up at 5 am. The washing went on and by six some of it was ready for the final rinse. There were no washing machines then, just plenty of elbow grease, a strong back and strong arms. Mum used two tubs, one for washing and one for rinsing. The only aids were the wooden dolly-peg, a scrubbing board and plenty of energy. Water was boiled in the kitchen copper, then carried to the tubs in a bucket. Some of the washing was boiled in the copper or in a large pan placed on the open coal fire.

All day long, Mum washed, dollied, scrubbed and rinsed. It all had to be perfect. Then she would dolly the blue and starch the whites, iron them and air them ready for wearing again. The two irons she used (I still have them) were hung on the fire grate until hot enough for ironing. She would test them by slightly spitting on them to see if they would hiss, then giving them a wipe with a piece of cloth. The washing, when it was all done, was neatly folded, put into the basket and ready for us to take back to the shop. By that time it was 9 p.m. Mum was paid half a crown – two shillings and sixpence: less than two pence an hour – for this long day's hard graft that was done with pride and skill.

Half a dollar, as it was known then, was not a lot of money for 15 hours' work, but for us it meant survival. It bought Dad 10 cigs and sixpence pocket money. He often told us not to send cigs or money to him, but Mum insisted. That's what love does for people. Tuesday dinner time I would go up the Co-op and get two stone of flour. Every Co-op, in every village, had a back room called the flour room, always manned by a young lad learning the trade. In each flour room, hanging from the ceiling, was a large shovel-shaped galvanised pan – a "weigh". This was used to weigh whatever was being bought. Around the room there was an assortment of box-type alcoves or drawers, containing Indian corn, wheat, bran, flour and a variety of other dried foods. The lad shovelled out whatever you wanted into the weigh until it reached the required weight. Then he would tip the scales and empty the contents into your bag or sack. I always used a white pillow case to fetch my flour in.

Having that two stone of flour was a Godsend to us. It meant that we always had some bread to eat and, with Mum's little extra earnings, something to put on it, be it marge, lard or a bit of dripping. Mum baked two or three times a week, making two, sometimes three, loaves and a dozen and a half oven bottom cakes. "Scufflers" we used to call them. We loved to eat them straight from the oven. Marvellous! Until you have eaten a nice home-baked loaf, fresh from the oven, you ain't tasted nothing yet!

# FIRST ENCOUNTER WITH THE LAW

Sadly, all this good fortune had to end. Some spiteful neighbour, perhaps a bit jealous of our little extra comfort, reported Mum for taking in washing. Along came the inquisitor from the Guardians of the Poor. Without even bothering to find out why my Mum had been 'earning money', he told her that while it wasn't a crime to work, it was a very serious crime to earn money and not declare it when she was being 'kept' by the Guardians who gave of their time and consideration so freely. She was admonished most brutally and told that she would be taken to Court and punished. Poor Mum; her world had come apart, her voucher had been stopped, how on earth was she going to feed her children? Even today, within our modern "welfare state", we still have such mindless insects, always on the lookout for a reason to stop a benefit because of their paranoia about scroungers.

Mum duly appeared at Court, frightened and with no one to help her, not knowing how to ask questions, and the silly Magistrate persistently asking if she had any questions to put to her accusers. He, with all due pomp and regard for the Guardians – such fine citizens – laid down the law, admonishing my beloved Mum and telling her she should feel ashamed of herself, and fined her £3.

Mum was already deeply ashamed; and how the hell did the Magistrate think she was going to pay a fine of £3? Did he not think for even a split second how a poor woman, working herself to the bone to feed and clothe four kids on seven shillings a week, would be able to pay a £3 fine? No: our well-fed, pompous Justice of the Peace fined her £3 – 1,300 hours of hard labour.

A few years later, I got to know the man, then approaching retirement. An ex-Trade Union official, and for his services to the system made a JP, and later bestowed with an honour from His Majesty. He was a also a frequent, indeed a most regular, attendant at the bar – the brewers' bar – where he would stick out his gut and loudly proclaim his faith in Socialism, the Trade Unions and the Labour Movement. I often watched him strutting around the village. He had bought a house in the better part of it. Always dressed in a black suit, gleaming fancy white shirt, black bow tie, a black homburg stuck on his head, and a big cigar stuck in his gob. The working class pillar of the establishment.

Anyway, to get on with my story, my Dad hurried home from the Sanatorium, to give what help he could to a sick and anxious woman. He got the weekly voucher back and a bit of cash added, on account of him being at home – a very sick man in need of extra food. Whenever Dad was at home he was allowed a free pint of milk and an egg each day. But no extra allowance for hungry kids. Every morning I went to the farm for the milk, but Dad left all the eggs until Sunday. On Sunday morning we each had a boiled egg for breakfast.

But there was still the problem of the £3 fine. Dad vowed he would never pay it. He would go down first. Several times the Police called, made all kinds of threats, but were always sent packing. "If you've got nowt, you can't pay owt," said my Dad. It was at this time that I learned a valuable lesson, which I applied many times in later years on behalf of debtors, workers on strike and many others feared about the Bailiffs.

Dad, knowing what was likely to happen, began to move out all the best bits of furniture we had. Puzzled about this, I asked my Mum why our sideboard was in Mrs Nicholson's. "Don't be nosey," she said, "they're just borrowing it." The sideboard, the sofa, the pictures on the wall, anything we didn't want to lose, were all farmed out to neighbours.

Then on Sunday, a minute after midnight – there was some law that said the Bailiff couldn't call on a Sunday, so they called at one minute past – there was a loud knock on the door. The Bailiff, escorted by two large bullies, walked in and set about collecting what bits of timber he could find. He knew what had happened, but there was nowt he could do about it. There were no carpets to rip up – we never had any – curtains were not worth taking, and so they bounced upstairs. And that was where my Dad had slipped up. He believed that beds could not be taken. But he was wrong. The beds were dismantled, the bedsteads and springs taken away, and only the mattresses left. They were not saleable. Mattresses at that time were mostly filled with feathers or straw. Perfect breeding grounds for fleas if they were not carefully cleaned and regularly changed. Mum was a stickler for that. For a while, until we could get some new bedsteads, we had to sleep on the floor. For Mum and Dad, it must have been soul-destroying. But for us kids it was an adventure, sleeping on the floor, jumping and romping around the bedroom. We all enjoyed it, and for a while saw it as lots of fun.

# LEARNING AND SURVIVING

My schooling was a hit and miss affair. There were many times when I was absent simply because I did not have clothes to go to school in. Throughout my school days, up to the age of 13, I never possessed more than one pair of trousers, one shirt, one pair of stockings and a jersey. I never enjoyed the luxury of having a pair of boots or shoes, except once when Mr Nicholson, a cobbler who lived next door to us, made me a pair for free. Once, too, I had a pair of second-hand shoes bought at a jumble sale. They were part-worn, but much better than the freezing-cold plimsolls I usually wore. The headmaster – the gaffer we called him; ex-army and always reminding us about it – was a stickler for having boots and shoes polished and shiny. He got very rough with the lads if their footwear looked a bit scruffy. Many times lads were in trouble, not because they didn't want to polish their boots or shoes, but because there was no polish at home to shine them with. It was the same for me, when I did have shoes. Every morning, because we didn't have polish, I would spit on my shoes and rub them with a soft cloth until I brought up a good shine. It didn't do the leather much good, but they got me through the winter. Mostly, I wore plimsolls. They were the only things I had to protect my feet in all weathers, come rain, snow or whatever. There were many times when my feet were cold and wet, and when it got too bad I had to stay at home and miss school.

It was because of my long absences from school that I learned how to make my own toys. I also spent long hours drawing, writing and, when I had paints, painting pictures. I became so good at copying landscapes, the gaffer would sometimes pull me out of lessons and set me on painting pictures which he would take away. I never saw them again.

One of my favourite pastimes was making my own toys. It was a really special occasion if I did have a toy bought for me. Sometimes at Christmas we would have some bought toys, but not always. Each week I would walk down to the quarry to scratch among the cinders for useful bits of wood, metal or anything else I could use. The quarry was where they had dug out the stone to build the stone houses within the area. It was now being used as a dump for cinders and household rubbish that could not be burned. There were times when I didn't find much that was of use to me, but there were other times when I would dig out a clockwork car or railway engine that had a broken spring. Some of them were in fairly good nick and became part of my collection of toys.

One of my passions was the building of my own working fairground. I had two sets of carousels that could turn around. I built them so that they would hang from a pivot which I stuck into the floor. The animals on the roundabouts were from bits of wood, metal or cardboard, hanging from the top circular ring on each roundabout. I had a few lead animals which I rescued from the quarry and some which I had won from the lads at marbles. I made a variety of dolly stalls, coconut stalls, and other fairground trappings. At the end of play I would dismantle the stalls and roundabouts and pack them into cardboard containers made like fairground vans. The vans were made from soap containers or other suitable small cardboard boxes. These I painted in bright colours after the fashion of the fairground caravans.

Food was often in short supply and there were times when, having no flour, Mum couldn't bake and we didn't even have a slice of bread to eat for breakfast. More than once, when I was sitting on the hot pipes in the school porch at playtime, the gaffer would ask me why I wasn't out playing. Sometimes I would tell him that I had a pain in my stomach. He would look at me and would ask "Have you had some breakfast this morning?" "No Sir," I would reply. "Well come along with me then." He would take me to his house, which was in the school grounds, and ask his wife to make me some breakfast. It was usually a bacon or egg sandwich and a nice hot cup of tea.

# LIVING OFF THE LAND

During the spring and early summer I roamed the hedgerows or climbed trees, finding birds' nests and looking for eggs. I had a strict code about the number of eggs I would take. Although I would feel a bit guilty about robbing the birds, I would console myself by always leaving some eggs in the nest. If there were only one or two eggs, I would leave them. If there were three eggs I would take one, and if there were four eggs, I would take two. I broke the eggs into my hand and drank them. I used to swallow about six or eight eggs; sometimes less, never more. Most of them were starlings'. I used to scrim up the drainpipes to get at them. Other eggs were hedge sparrows', blackbirds' or thrushes'. They were plentiful and easy to get to. Sometimes I managed to get to a magpie's nest, but because they were usually high in a hawthorn tree I would finish up with my hands and wrists in scratches. Now and again I could manage a crow's nest, but that was risky because the branches at that height would sway and bend a lot. I remember one day very clearly. I was climbing to get to a storm cock's nest. All the way up the tree one of the birds flew at me, trying to peck at my face. Back and forth it flew, doing its very best to stop me climbing. As I got close enough to the nest to look in his mate had a go at me too. Then I saw four wide-open mouths screeching for food and was only too glad to beat a hasty retreat.

The next phase of my food hunting would be the orchards. There were five farms in the village, and all had well stocked orchards. But the biggest and the best was Ritchies', only a couple of hundred yards across the field from where I lived. It had a fine variety of different grades of apples, pears, plums, and cherries. One tree was my favourite: always packed with smallish apples, a pale green colour. And the taste? It was sort of pineapple-sweet and soft in texture, with a lovely fragrance and very juicy. I have never since tasted an apple so delicate in flavour and so honeysome. I used to collect around twenty apples to take home for the kids and they lasted us a couple or three days. There were also a couple of really good bramleys, and once a week I would fetch two or three of these apples home. Mum would then make us a delicious apple pie. While the bramleys lasted there was always a thick delicious apple pie for Sunday tea. There were times also when we had blackberry pie.

A lot of the lads raided the orchards as we did, but they would do it mostly for mischief. They would pull as many as they could, take a bite and then hurl them at each other. But I only took what I needed for Mum and the kids. I wanted them to last. When the apples were gathered in by the farmer, I would sometimes go to the farm and buy a few, if I had a penny. Old Ritchie, a genial sort of bloke, would pile me up with as many apples as he could load into my rolled-up jersey.

By this stage of the year I had started pulling wheat. I would go into the fields and pull off the ears of it and then, taking it and blowing into my cupped hands to separate the chaff and blow it away, I would eat the grain. I didn't know this at the time, but I was eating one of the finest foods there is, and in the best possible way.

My other regular food was the swede, although we always called them turnips or "tongies". I remember one day, when I must have been about eight, I had been into the quarry but there wasn't much to salvage. So I walked up the road for about a mile and came across a field of turnips. I pulled one, screwed off the top leaves and rubbed the base on a stone to clean the soil from it. Then I began to bite off the thick peel so that I could eat it. Suddenly I was scared out of my wits by a loud voice yelling, "What the effing hell do you think you are up to?" Then, wham! I felt his fist hit me twice. I staggered back, reeling into the ground. I got up trembling and in pain. "I'm only having a turnip," I said. "Well bloody get off!" yelled the farmer, like a demon from hell, his red face turning purple. "And if I see you up here again I'll ring your bleeding neck."

I went home, and as I walked into the house, my Mum looked at my face, exclaiming, "Oh my lad, who's done that to you?" My face by now had swollen and was hurting quite a bit. Looking again, she went on "You've got a reit black eye lad. Let me bathe it for you." While she was doing this, I told her what happened. By this time my Dad had come in. He looked at my face and asked who had done it. I told him the farmer had done it because I was pinching a turnip. "Right," he said. "I'm going up there and I'll black his bloody eyes. He's not doing that to my lad and getting away with it."

My Dad, and Mum with him, set off to the field. Neighbours found out what had happened and before we had walked no more than 20 yards, half a dozen blokes and around a dozen women had joined us. And what they were going to do when they got hold of that farmer doesn't bear repeating. Away we marched, with me feeling quite proud of my shiner.

By the time we entered the field, the talk had developed into laughter and jokes about the various extremities of the farmer and what they would do with them.

As we entered the field, the farmer saw us coming. He tried to make off, but was too late. We closed in around him, and my Dad grabbed hold of him, saying "Look what you have done to my lad, just for one lousy turnip". And then, wallop, Dad hit him twice. He went down and wouldn't get up again. Full of contempt for his cowardice, we all set off home. About an hour later the farmer rode into the yard where we lived, along with the local bobby, both on their bikes. The bobby, a big fat-bellied bloke, demanded, in a pompous hostile manner, to know who had assaulted the farmer, and promised what would happen to the culprit when he was identified. By now, neighbours had gathered round and told the bobby that the farmer had got what he deserved. Then Dad stepped forward saying, with some anger, "Yes, I thumped him. And if he touches my lad again, I'll thump him again." Then, holding me forward, he said to the bobby, "See what he's done to my lad. What you going to do about that?" The bobby looked at my face, which was purple, badly swollen and with one eye closed. He said nowt; just turned to the farmer, muttered something to him, and they both got on their bikes and rode off to loud cheers from the neighbours.

To get back to my diet. One of my foods, when better stuff was not available, was roots and catnuts. For quite a while I had been chewing the roots from the hawthorn, which was the main structure for the hedgerows around the fields. They weren't very tasty – a bit acid really, dry and difficult to chew, soon turning into a sort of dry pulp. But dotted among the hawthorns were a number of hazelnut trees. Some of them fruited and I ate nuts from many of them. Once, when there were no nuts available, I tried the roots. Can't say they were very tasty, but they were quite chewable and a bit juicy, not bad at all really. I used to cut a root, a little bit thicker than a pencil, and chop it into pieces about an inch long. It was while I was digging around one day that I found some round nut-like pods. I don't know what they were, but I tried one. It was very much like a nut, but not quite as hard; very sweet and tasty. They were for a time part of my regular food. The kids liked them too. There were times when they were hard to find, but there was always summat else to have a go at.

# GRANDMA K

Grandma K, my Dad's Ma, lives vividly in my memory. She had that sort of character, commonplace maybe in those days, which our writers and television producers would love to have today. But they are harder to find now.

Gran looked to me as if she was old as Adam, but that was because I was just a nipper. At the time, she was twenty or more years younger than I am today. I remember her best when she sat in her rocking chair by a blazing coal fire smoking her clay pipe. She was always dressed in a long black frock, almost touching the floor, and was never without a man's flat cap stuck on her head. She had a strong, broad, Yorkshire accent, and was blunt and direct in her speech, especially if she was having 'words' with someone. But in spite of this, she was mostly gentle, caring and generous. Everybody in the village knew her, and many of them called upon her for help or advice if they had problems. She was famous for her knowledge and skill with herbs. Aperitifs, tonics, laxatives, she could make them all, and her cough mixture? They all swore by it.

It was because of her skill with people and their ailments that she saved my life one day. Gran lived at the bottom end of the village in a single row of 16 terraced houses. The village consisted of small communities like this one, scattered around a large area. These houses were a bit isolated from the rest. Most of the land around them was marshy, situated in a kind of valley between rising land on either side. Because of this there were a number of open sewers, each about 20 feet in length and 10 feet wide. A small brick wall two feet high encased each sewer. I was six years old at the time. I had been to visit Gran; then I went playing around the sewers and was walking along the top of one of the walls. Suddenly I lost my balance and fell into the sewer. Luckily for me, there were three men and a couple of youths nearby. Within an instant, they fished me out, coughing, spluttering and fit to burst. The men hurried me to Gran's, fifty yards away. She took hold of me, gave me something to drink and made me vomit. She undressed me, bathed me and dressed me up in a pair of knitted green trousers and jumper – more for a girl than a boy. I was disgusted at having to wear these things. She gave me a dose of one of her herbal drinks, and made me sit by the fire until she was ready to take me home.

Next morning I went to school protesting loudly and indignantly because I had to wear the horrible green knitted suit. But I had to go. Half way through morning lessons, I felt an urgent need to go the toilet, but the teacher ignored my desperate pleas and told me to wait until playtime. Lots of kids had to suffer this kind of treatment in those days. I begged, I pleaded, but the teacher yelled "No." Getting desperate, holding myself rigid, I dared not move, dared not even breathe, holding myself tense and squeezing my buttocks tightly. Then it happened, to my horror and shame, diarrhoea simply bubbled out of me – soiled the desk seat, filled my trousers, ran down my legs and into my socks and slippers. What a dreadful state I was in! How could I ever live down such humiliation? I was packed off home. Walking homewards, I would have been grateful if the ground could have opened up and swallowed me.

Mum looked at me, "Oh, my poor lad, what happened to you?" She comforted me and bathed me. "Anyway Joey, your clothes have been washed and you can put them on now." As I dressed, Mum made me a hot pot of tea and a couple of slices of bread and jam. Felt a lot better after that.

Gran was also noted for her skill in delivering babies. There were no official midwives for our village at that time. When women were expecting, Gran would be sent for. I remember once, when the woman two doors away was in pain and thought she was due at any moment, she called "Go down and fetch thi Grandma, tell her to come straight away!" I went down to Gran's, gave her the message: "Tha's to come straight away," I said.

Gran, knocking her pipe out, took hold of a small leather bag and said "Come on then lad, I'll bet she's got wind up for nowt, it's allus same." I walked up with Gran, and being a noddy little bugger, I followed her into the house and stayed very quiet – 'earwigging'.

Gran took a good look at the woman and in her usual gruff manner, said: "Tha can stop bloody moaning, tha not due yet. I'll tell thi when tha ready." Gran took off her coat, pulled a chair up by the fire, pulled out a twist of black chewing tobacco, and using her sharp small penknife, with the twist protruding from between her fingers, she deftly cut off thin slices of the twist, rubbed them between her palms and packed them into her clay pipes. While she was smoking, she saw me standing quietly by. "And thee, buggerlugs, hop it!" And I did, sharply.

Gran had another job in the village. If anyone was fished out of the canal or found dead Gran was sent for. Her job? To wash and lay out the corpse ready for the undertaker and other officials who might want to take a look. The bodies were taken into the stables at the back of the local pub. There, a long black coffin-shaped wooden board was placed on two trestles, and the corpse was laid on it. Helping her, my first job was to fetch water in buckets from the pub; then to help with the washing of the corpse. It was never a pleasant task, but for my help Gran would give me a penny. Some of the bodies were not too bad, but others, especially if they had been in the canal for two or three days, were foul and revolting, and stank to high heaven. One of the things I soon learned about a corpse, was the colour and texture of the skin in different parts of the body. And how cold the whole body was. The forehead always seemed to be iron hard. Other areas of the body were cold, clammy and viscous, and something like the texture of putty but not as pliable. The colour of the bodies varied from a dark apple green to a sort of lemon green. Ugly, vile really, and what a tragedy it seemed for humans to end up in this state. One memory that always sticks with me was when I was washing a man. I half turned his body so that I could wipe his back, and he broke wind. I hurriedly backed away from him, struggling to get my breath. I thought I was going to choke. Once outside, I sat on a bench near the stable door.

Gran came out: "Ah tha alreet Joey?"

"Yes Gran."

She gave me a penny, "Go an get thissen some spice," she said.

There is no way I can describe the stink of that moment, and no way that I can ever forget it.

# MY DAD

My Dad was a well-built man, broad in the shoulders and well developed in the limb. He was taller than I am, nearly 5' 9". My brothers were also taller than me. I'm what you might call the shorty of the family. My physique was after the style of my Dad though – even stronger because of the years I spent in the gym. My Doctor, who was also a keen physical culturist, sometimes let me use his own private gym. He used to say to me that I was built like a tank, and nicknamed me the pocket battleship or a pocket Hercules.

During the 1914 war, Dad served in the infantry and was damaged in a gas raid while in France. He was later discharged from the Army, but was denied a war pension on the grounds that his disability was caused by tuberculosis, not by the gassing. This is typical of the British Government, which always seeks to dodge its responsibilities towards those who lost their lives or were disabled by actions forced upon them in the interests of the state

When Dad was discharged he went back to the pit, the last place he should have gone to. It wasn't long before he became ill again because of tuberculosis. Before long he was in and out of sanatoriums and unable to resume heavy work. Like Grandma, he knew quite a lot about herbs, but he only used them as food or for making refreshing drinks. He taught me a little about these things and sometimes took me out looking for herbs. One of the things he taught me, and which I did for many years, was to dig up and select the roots of bulrushes, dry them into hard sticks, and then chew them. They were wonderful for helping your breathing, especially if you were involved with boxing, wrestling and other hard physical exercise. I enjoyed walking out with him and listening to him explaining about the different plants and herbs. He used to walk the fields very often because getting plenty of fresh air was part of his treatment.

He also spent a lot of time fishing.

He was well known for his knowledge and skill in catching fish. Many tried to match him, but couldn't. He had his own secrets which he guarded jealously. John Brady, a well-known grocer with a number of shops around Barnsley, often asked Dad to take him fishing, especially when he was trying to catch pike and wanted to pick up a few secrets from him. Whenever Dad and Brady went fishing, old Brady, because he had pots of money, always preferred to use goldfish as bait. Yet somehow he was never able to catch the big ones as Dad did. Dad could not afford goldfish; he didn't want them anyway. He used minnows. He would take me three or four miles across the fields, to a quiet patch of the River Dearne. There were loads of minnows there, ideal for pike fishing. Minnows are beautiful sleek little fish that grow to four or five inches. Dad always chose the shorter ones because, he told me, the younger and shorter ones were less able to get away from the marauding pikes. Brady believed the bigger the goldfish, the better the chance of getting a bite. He wouldn't learn.

Besides pike, Dad fished for roach, carp, bream, perch and eels. They were always sought after by the neighbours as a cheap source of food. Some he would give away; for others he might ask for a few cigs. The large ones, especially the pike, he would sell to Edgars the butcher or to Mrs Bill at the fish and chip shop. I used to love eating the pike and the perch. The perch isn't much to look at, but the taste? Unforgettable!

One of my jobs was to go along to the Edgars, usually on Tuesdays, and take a couple of gallon cans. Edgar, because he knew what I had come for, let me into the slaughterhouse at the bottom of the yard. Inside the slaughterhouse and fastened to the wall, was a steel ring about 8 inches in diameter. When he was killing a beast he would fasten a rope round its neck, lead it into the slaughterhouse, and get one of his helpers to thread the rope through the steel ring, and pull the beast up to it. Edgar would stand at the ring, waiting for the beast. He had in his hands a seven pound hammer. At the hitting end there was a protrusion about two inches long and about a quarter of an inch in diameter. As the beast's head was pulled up to the ring, Edgar would make one mighty blow into the forehead of the beast, and slap! the animal hit the floor. Then Edgar would slit its throat, and a couple of helpers would push and press the beast to make the blood flow more quickly. It was my job to catch the blood and fill my two-gallon cans. When the blood gushed out I could feel the heat of it, and the smell. Sometimes it would make me feel quite sick.

When I got the blood home, Dad would put the cans in a specially prepared corner in the field at the back of the house. They were left there until the blood had turned into a thick black-red jelly. When he was going to fish for eels he would take one can of the jellied blood to his chosen place and feed the waters with it for several nights. When the night came for his fishing he would take two rods, the eels were ready and he couldn't pull them out quick enough. Next morning he would give the small eels to some of the neighbours who used to relish them. The big ones he would skin, and hang the skins on the wall outside until they had dried out. People would buy them to wear around their waists under their clothes. They vowed they were the best relief for rheumatics they had ever tried. The other can of blood Dad would dry into a fine powder by some process known only to him. He would use this for colouring his maggots and the groundbait. Always, before fishing, he would feed the river with groundbait, and keep feeding it when he was fishing. He doused his minnows with the same powder when fishing for pike.

Some of the best days I can remember were those when Dad took me fishing. One beautiful day a friend of his took us up to the River Nidd on his motor bike and side car. As always, I made a small fire from bits of wood. More than once, when Dad pulled out a decent looking perch, he would hand it to me, saying: "Here thy are lad." And within minutes it was gutted, cleaned and cooking on my fire. However grand and sumptuous the expensive dinners of the rich and powerful may be, they have nothing to compare to the flavour and pleasure which that little perch gave me on the banks of the Nidd.

# THE PIGEON

I made frequent visits to the quarry to look for oddments – broken toys, anything that might be useful. On this day, a fine summer's day it was, I was leaving the quarry when I saw a pigeon, sitting still and quiet on the grass verge beside the road. I stopped, looked at the pigeon, and then carefully walked towards it. It never moved at all, and I wondered if it was dead. Feeling a bit anxious for it, I touched it and discovered to my horror that it had a hole torn under its breast. "Poor little bird," I said to it. I cried for it, thinking it must be in terrible pain. "You've been shot," I said. But I could see that it was alive. I took off my jersey and gently cradled the pigeon within it and, holding it as gently as I could, I hurried home. I wanted to run, but daren't in case I hurt it.

When I got home, I told Mum what I had found and asked her to have a look at it.

"What can you do for it Mum," I asked.

"Don't know." Then after a pause, she said, "Take it down to your uncle Jack. He knows all about pigeons. He'll tell you what to do."

Uncle Jack lived nearly three miles away, so off I hurried, half crying and full of anxiety for the poor little thing. I could almost feel the pain for it. After what seemed like an endless journey, I got to Uncle Jack's house. He had just come in from the pit and was having his dinner. I showed him the pigeon and pleaded with him to make it better.

"Allreight Joey lad." And, getting up from the table, he took hold of the pigeon and gently, ever so gently, examined it, opening its wings.

"They look allreight." Then he saw the hole in the pigeon's breast. "Aye," he muttered. "Looks as though she has cot herself on some barbed wire or summat. It can't be reight bad though Joey lad, or she'd be dead by now." Then he turned to my aunt Helen, his wife. "Get me a fine needle and some cotton luv." She opened a tin box, got out a needle and threaded some cotton through it. Then uncle Jack gave the pigeon to me, saying, "Hold it like this Joey lad, and keep still." Then he put in about eight stitches which sealed the hole.

"There," he said, "That's all I can do for it. Tek it home and put it somewhere quiet, an I'll come and have a look at her tomorrow." He gave me a large shoe-box , put in some soft down, and settled the pigeon on to it.

I walked home feeling a lot better and talked to the pigeon all the way. "You'll get better, you'll get better," I kept saying, and gave her a gentle kiss on her head. Uncle Jack had also fetched some pigeon food from a neighbour, saying "Put some o' this in her box and a drop of water."

When I got home I sorted out a quiet corner in the house and put her where she would not be disturbed. I just sat looking at her, praying for her to get better. For hours and hours I sat, just looking and praying. Next day Uncle Jack came up. "Aye," he said, "She dun't look so bad. Keep her here for a couple o' day an I'll come up an' look at her again. Go to t'shop and get a couple of apple boxes an I'll make a little hut for her. Ah wish thi Dad had been home. He'd done this for thee; he's better than me at this game."

I went to the shop and got a couple of apple boxes and knocked together a small hut with a perch, and fixed a door, using some old soft leather tongues from a pair of old boots as hinges. By this time the pigeon was showing signs of recovery. I knew this because I could see droppings, which meant she was feeding. I made her comfortable in the little hut that I had made. I went up to the farm and got some good clean hay to make the hut warm. By the next day, she was on the perch and cooing a bit. I went down to tell Uncle Jack that she was cooing and flipping her wings.

"Well in that case," he said, "you'd better leave the door open in the morning, so that if she wants to come out, she will be able to do so.

"But she'll fly away," I protested in alarm.

"Well Joey lad, if she wants to fly, you'll have to let her go."

"But I'll lose her," I cried.

"Well she might not fly away, but if she does, it means that she has got a family to go back to. You wouldn't want to keep her away from her family, would you? What if you got lost? You'd want to go home again – eh?"

"Aye, I would, but I don't want to lose her, I can look after her."

"You can't lock her up Joey lad, it would be cruel."

"I'll leave the door open in't morning then."

Next morning I left the door open for her, put in some food and changed the water, then went off to school, praying like mad she would be there when I got back home. I raced home as fast as I could after school, and she was still there perched on top of the hut. Oh, what a relief! On the third day, when I got home, she was missing. My heart was broken, and I cried. Then all of a sudden, she came flying down, stood on the hut for a short while, cooing and stretching her wings. What a happy feeling it was. She loved me, I know she loved me. Then she flew on to my shoulder, cooing all the time.

After a minute, her wings flipped my cheek and then she flew off. High up into the sky she flew, circled round, and went out of sight, but still in my heart. I knew I had lost her, and I began to cry. Mum came out to me. Putting her arms around me, she said: "Don't cry love, you did save her life you know, and now she has gone home to her family."

For a long time, whenever I saw pigeons circling the sky, as they often did, I looked up and wondered to myself. Is she up there flying with them? I liked to think that she was.

# THE MINERS' LOCKOUT, 1926

This is not the place to go into the whys and wherefores of the miners' strike.[1] I will just tell you how the strike affected me, my family and the surrounding communities.

I have said a little about the poverty that my family and others suffered at this time: how we were always short of food, clothing and all the other things that we needed. The supply was there in the shops, to be looked at wistfully: but we had no money to pay for these things. Even those in work were mostly in poverty – especially the miners. Pay was low, work was hard and dangerous, and sickness and accidents took their toll. And work was not always regular, especially in summer time when demand for coal fell and part-time working became the rule. For those who were unemployed or unable to work, life was simply degrading.

As a family – and there were many others like us – we never knew where the next meal was coming from. And when we did have a meal, it was never enough. For breakfast, it was a couple of thick slices of bread. If we were lucky we had a splodge of dripping to put on it; sometimes it was lard, others, nowt except for a sprinkling of sugar. And there were times when we didn't even have that. Sometimes, when Dad was at home, things were a bit better. He could get a bit of work now and again and the pressures were eased. But the little money he earned was soon swallowed up in getting the things a family needed if life was to be worth living. While we did get a bit more to eat, other things were missing. Footwear, warm clothing, blankets for the bed were always in short supply, sometimes not there at all. The warmest clothing we ever had for the bed was Dad's old Army greatcoat and a couple of other coats.

When Dad was away things got really bad. There was no money, just a food voucher which could be spent only on food. Having to buy a bar of soap, a towel or even a pair of stockings, meant less to be spent on food. Many's the time I have wondered, how the hell did we manage? Breakfast was almost non-existent, dinner not much better; a heap of mashed potatoes and swede, cabbage and a sort of gravy made out of Oxo. A woman with kids to feed in those times had to be a genius. If there happened to be any real meat, it was a special saved for Sunday. A

Yorkshire pudding helped the medicine go down, but for that Mum needed eggs, and eggs, like bacon, were things to dream about. It wasn't so much what you had to eat; it was whether the belly was full or not. Sometimes there was a bit of a home-caught fish and a few chips, or a bit of jam for the bread, but those were treats.

For the rest, what could a Mother do with a bloody food voucher that was geared, not to providing enough food and nourishment but to provide the minimum required to keep us from starving: enough to keep you alive, but never enough to allow you to live in dignity and peace of mind?

Then along came the strike, and a long-suffering strike it was to be. Except that it wasn't a strike, it was a lockout by the pit owners. Men could only go back to work if they accepted a cut in wages and an increase in working time. "Not a penny off the pay, not a minute on the day," was their slogan. What kind of man worth his salt could accept these terms when working conditions and rates of pay were already so bad? They were locked out for a long time, 28 weeks – and even then were not ready to give in and accept defeat if they had not been let down by the union leaders.

July 1926 – Half page advert in Barnsley Chronicle

Many men were prosecuted and fined for no real offence. Any attempt at picketing at a "day 'ole" a few miles away, where scabs were working, was subject to baton charges by thugs dressed in Bobbies' clothes. Some men were taken in and fined as much as £40 for trivial offences. Yes – we knew who the enemy was in those days. Baton-charging bobbies, well trained and treating the men as though they were animals fit only for slaughter. Heavy fines were imposed by the Justices, knowing full well that the fines could never be paid, and that would eventually mean prison.

Many were fined for just scratching for coal on the pit mud stacks, "stealing coal", they called it. How could they call it stealing, when they were digging bloody hard for the stuff that had been thrown away to make eyesores for the community? One Sunday afternoon, aged eleven, I went along with around a dozen neighbours to some nearby railway sidings that were being built. They were fetching wagonloads of pit muck to build up the site for the sidings. Naturally there were bits of coal among the muck. The men went down to pick out coal from it and they had hardly got started when, out of the blue, came the men in blue. Dark blue uniforms of bobbies, wielding pickaxes looking as ugly as they were. Ready and more than willing to knock hell out of poor blokes that just wanted to make a bit of fire for their kids. And they laid into the men with the ugly intent of crippling them. I could almost hear their bones cracking as they tried to fight back. But at about 5 to 1 the men had no chance. They were carted off to prison, tried and fined. Meantime I was crouched in a wagon, terrified. I had peeped over the edge of the wagon, watched the brutality happen, then got back into the corner of it and tried to hide myself behind a big piece of rock. The bobbies were climbing into the wagons to look for other men. Eventually they got to the one I was in. I saw a helmet, then a face, appear over the wagon top. Then a wild, yelling voice shouted: "Out, OUT, get your bloody self out of there." I climbed out of the wagon, shaking nervously, "I'm not doing owt wrong," I said. He slapped my face and growled at me, "Get off home, and if I see you down here again, you will get what that lot just had."

Later I made me a trolly ("cadgies", we called them) out of a flat piece of wood, about two feet by one, with four wheels, and a rope to pull it. Then I went to an old disused railway belonging to the pit. I dug into the sides of the embankment looking for bits of coal. I had an old army kitbag and a small sandbag, which I filled after an hour or two's digging. As well as for our own use, I fetched coal for Mrs Nicholson next door. Her husband was a disabled ex-serviceman. He used to get about in a wheelchair which had been fixed up with gears and a chain, so that he could pedal the chair with his hands. He had no legs. Because he had to move his chair using only his hands and arms, he developed shoulders and arms like Hackensmidt (a Russian weight lifter of the time). He got a grant from the Government and set himself up as a cobbler. It was he who made me the pair of clogs so that I could go to school. When I left school at 14, to work down the pit, he made me a second pair so that I could start work.

We were always half starved and without enough clothing. The shops were full of food, clothes and all the things a family needs. But not for the likes of us. The nearest we ever got to them was to stare wistfully at them in the shop window.

When the lockout started things changed, at least for the kids. Now the whole mining community was under attack, not just the isolated families without workers. Because of the harshness of the work and the hardships the miners suffered, and because of the close community bond between them, the pressure to go back to work under even worse conditions was not as heavy as it might have been. I remember my Dad and others calling the return to work a "betrayal". They were angry. They felt let down and they wanted to fight on. Just think about it: an extra three hours a week of hard labour, and around a dollar a week (5 shillings) out of the pay tin. (Miners at that time received their wages in coins dropped in a small tin cup).

We could have carried on, and most of the mining communities felt the same way. A new alternative economy and culture had been set up. The problem of being wageless had in many respects been solved. New forms of organised and spontaneous community action emerged. Trades Councils and Trade Unions, along with the people, set up effective soup kitchens where a good dinner and tea were provided every day for the kids. For the first time in my life I learned what it was like to get a regular meal.

There were no worries about the rent: the rent man didn't call no more! Apart from those who were not on strike, there was no income, and so no rent could be collected. Debt collectors and insurance men had stopped calling. Baliffs were outwitted. We weren't pestered in those days with all the modern paraphernalia of debts for cars, mortgages and all the other ersatz trappings of the so-called good life. An isolated family in rent arrears can be made to suffer, but you can't punish the whole flaming village when they are all in the same boat. So why bother about debt?

It couldn't last. After the strike, rents were increased by 6d or 9d to help clear the arrears. The Board of Guardians provided limited help for distressed families, but they had to watch it. Some Guardians were threatened with prosecution for being too generous or bending the rules. But for 28 weeks, within the common bond created by shared hardship, a new-found culture of social and community living emerged. The people didn't need professionals to teach them how to organise their lives. They dealt with reality, not theory. The men and women of the community knew what was needed, and they got on with it. First they organised the soup kitchens. The children were the first priority. They had to be fed, and for this, they needed money. With the organising skills of the Trades Councils and local Miners' Unions they raised it. Our soup kitchen was set up in the local church hall. Many of the women volunteered. Indeed the organisers were spoiled for choice. They prepared and cooked the food, waited at table and did all the work demanded by a boisterous mob of hungry kids. A good dinner and a good tea were there every day.

Hallelujah: the hungry days were over! Now that Mum didn't have to get a dinner or tea for us, we could get a bit of breakfast as well. Many people and organisations sent in food or donations, usually from other unions or people who cared, and the good ole Co-op was in the front with its aid. After all, the Co-op is the peoples' shop, and very much so in those days. In addition, every village organised its own cash-raising events and food collection and distribution points.

At weekends, Galas and Carnivals were organised and many thousands of pounds were raised. A typical carnival, especially in the larger villages, provided a day of sports and social fun for the kids and for the grown ups. Fancy dress or comic dress parades and competitions were held. There were sprint races for kids and for old men, slow cycle races, races with a wheelbarrow with a big bloke sat in it dressed as a baby and sucking a big dummy, egg and spoon races, greasy poles to climb with a ham on top for the first one who could get to it. Skipping and skipping races, bowling at the wicket, men's football and women's cricket: these were real fun games we could all take part in and enjoy. Some of the carnivals were attended by as many as ten thousand people.

Most of the pit villages had their own comic band. Many of them – a dozen at least – would come to the carnivals. These bands paraded round the villages where carnivals were being held, to be followed by a comic band contest. The most common instrument played, was the kazoo, or "tommy talker" as we called them. My Uncle Tom was the leader of our comic band with his concertina, helped by Martin Homer who played the accordion. We were lucky enough to have a big drum, and one bloke had a bugle. Real instruments were hard to come by and the men made music with whatever they could get – old pans and dustbin lids along with the kazoos; owt that would make a noise. Pitmen, with their wives and kids, wearing home-made fancy dress, marched proudly behind their bands, singing and having fun. I still have vivid memories of as many as twenty bands parading around the village. After the strike many villages continued with their annual carnivals right up to the war of 1939.

One of the best bands had real instruments. Two of its members blacked their bodies and dressed in straw skirts as Zulu warriors. Women and kids shrieked as they charged at them with raised spears, whooping, grimacing and yelling out a noise I don't know how to write. These were wonderful, happy days, showing how good life can be, despite hardships, when people forget their worries and join with others to live and play together in harmony.

Mum played in the women's cricket team for the village. They won through to the final of a knockout competition which was to be played in our own village park, chosen because it had an excellent pitch. The women always played their games dressed in mens' pyjamas. On the day of the final, some women came to our house to get dressed for the game. I was booted out of the way while they got changed, but I can remember them now, laughing out loud and joking about the "jamas". I can only guess what they were joking about. I had never seen a pair of pyjamas before; indeed I didn't even know they existed.

And all these events raised brass, and brass got food for the kids. The food may not have been fancy, but it was wholesome and plentiful, and hungers were satisfied. Dinners were a mixture of fresh meats or stews, with the usual veg, and sometimes rice pudding or treacle pudding. When puddings were served they always got a big hooray. Sometimes it was an apple or orange, or both. For tea, it was usually sandwiches of corned beef, potted beef, or cheese salads. And sometimes there were banana sandwiches, with a slab of currant cake and cream buns, and many hoorays. It was always good to get out of school and chase off to the kitchen, and look forward to a good satisfying meal.

Indeed, they were exciting times, especially when we arrived before the doors were open. There would be a great huddle of kids, shouting, hustling, singing or chanting: "Open up, open up!" – lively, friendly and noisy. I can still smell the tea brewing, pea soup and all the other aromas of food cooking – smells that torture hungry kids ready for a good bust up.

One of my fondest memories, were the warm summer evenings when all the neighbours gathered in the yard, sitting around on bricks or chairs. Uncle Tom would play his concertina, Martin Homer his accordion, and someone would drag out a piano. They all sang and laughed and danced until three in the morning. It was at that time that I learned my favourite waltz: "Three o'clock in the Morning, we'll dance the Whole Night Through."

Then one day the lockout ended. Men went back to work for longer hours and reduced pay: back to the old struggle and strife. At least for a time. But things did eventually get better. When you are at the bottom of the pile, there's only one way to go.

# BEGGING

The thought of people having to beg in a wealthy society always sickens and angers me. I reckon that my feelings are prompted by my own early years of deprivation. None of it was my fault or my parents' fault. We lived in a world where, even now, it's dog eat dog. My family's poverty was caused by the greed, indifference and neglect of the ruling class. Poverty, like accidents, doesn't just happen; it is caused. The deprived are deprived because they are treated as objects, not as people.

Once, when I was a ragged-arsed nipper, I had been away from school for a while because I didn't have footwear fit for me to go to school in. Mum was anxious and worried for me. In desperation one day she gave me a sealed envelope to take to the big house, t'other side of the village. The house was a large one with two great big bay windows at the front, one on each side of thick double doors. It was surrounded by a seven-foot brick wall, with ugly slivers of broken glass along the top, enclosing half an acre of grounds. I knew there were dogs there, because I heard them barking sometimes when I passed the house. There was a thick, ten-foot-wide wooden gate, high as the wall, bolted and barred inside; and at the side of this gate a door to allow people through.

When I got to the gate I opened the side door and looked anxiously for any signs of the dogs. I couldn't see any, so I entered and walked nervously along the drive and towards the front doors. As I got near the door two great dogs rushed up, mouthing and barking savagely, both of them twice the size of me. One of them, foaming at the mouth, stuck his great paws on my chest, shoving me flat against the wall. I stood back, rigid with fright. The hot foul breath of the growling dog on my face made me sick. Somehow, after some wriggling against the wall, I got to the house bell rope, pulled it, and after a while and much to my relief, a maid came. She sent the dogs away, took the envelope from me and disappeared. I waited, terrified lest the dogs might return. Some ten minutes later, the maid came back and gave me a parcel.

I hurried home wondering what the parcel contained. Mum opened the parcel and I saw what was inside. An almost new pair of boys' trousers, made from a very fine black and white checked material, a pale blue jersey, a pair of expensive white slippers, stockings and a cricket shirt. There were also a few other oddments – fancy cakes, biscuits and bread. I screamed at Mum: "You sent me begging!" I ran outside and away across the fields a long way. Walking at last, then sitting, I wondered what to do. It was getting late; tired and hungry, I felt sorry for shouting at Mum. It was growing dark and I began to feel a bit nervous for I didn't know where I was. I found my way home and could see that Mum had been crying. A neighbour a couple of doors away had put her up to it, she said, but she would never do it to me again.

To beg and not to fight back was to accept your place in life – a lesson I had already learnt. This and other events in my childhood instilled in me a hatred for any kind of charity. Charity and handouts are given to drunks on skid row. They should not be for decent, respectable victims of an uncaring society and its Government. Trickling down cast-offs from the wealthy to the poor through charity is an offensive way to redistribute wealth. People who organise charity believe they are doing good, but they maintain poverty and injustice. In essence, their actions are criminal, for they take part in a theft that punishes the less fortunate.

Anyway, Mum sweetly encouraged me to try on the clothes, saying lovingly: "You'll be able to go to school tomorrow". The clothes fitted me perfectly and I felt wonderful in them. By now Mum and I were very chummy and happy again. She made me a cup of tea and a bit of supper, and, looking at me with a smile, she said: "You look very smart luv".

Next morning I went off to school like a new man: full of energy and feeling good. It was really wonderful to feel that I was well dressed. Arriving at the school, I walked into the classroom and Gaffer Slack, the headmaster, looked at me quizzically and remarked: "You're looking smart this morning Kenyon". I sat at my desk feeling that I wanted to do my best. Half way through the morning, I was working on a composition with a new nib in my pen and writing as best I could – a copperplate style of writing which I was good at. During my long periods of absence from school I used to spend hours and hours drawing and writing. After a while I felt Gaffer Slack looking down at me. Without speaking he bent over and took hold of my exercise book and left the classroom.

My mate Titch nudged me, saying "Nar then, what's tha been up to Joey?" "Nowt" I said.

"Well, what's he taken thi book for?"

"I dunt know, he didn't say owt."

After a while Gaffer Slack returned. He told us all to parade in the big room. At the front of the room, he had fixed up a blackboard, and on the board there were two open exercise books. The Gaffer ordered everybody to walk past the board and take a good look at the writing. The first book had a dirty smudged page of bad writing with lots of ink blots. The second book showed a page of neat, clean copperplate writing. And as the boys passed the second book, he ordered them to take a good look, saying: "This is how I want you all to write in future." Then he praised me for my wonderful writing. I had spent many hours at home practising my writing and because I felt so good in my new clothes the work seemed a lot easier for me somehow.

# THE BUTCHER

One other job I developed during those bleak years was shopping at Edgar's, the butcher. Every Saturday evening I went to Edgar's to get six penn'orth of pie bits, – a low-grade stewing meat. I learned over time that if I went late on a Saturday, and waited until old Edgar got back from his round, I could get a lot more for my money. And so, from about 8.30 in the evening, I waited about by the shop window and watched for Edgar coming home, always with one eagle eye on the shop and one on the road to make sure I didn't miss him.

Every Saturday morning old Edgar set off on his rounds delivering joints around our village and the neighbouring village. He used to travel on his pony and trap, and on the way he made one or two calls for his favourite tipple. His final call was at the Railway Hotel. He got there about three o'clock, had a bite of lunch and then sat knocking them back until about 8.30 p.m. or a bit later.

He finished up in a right old state, singing merrily and letting the pony find its own way home. When they got home the pony would stop at the gates leading down into the yard and the stables. There I used to wait and see what happened. If his son came out and took the pony down into the yard I knew that Edgar would go into the shop in a right jolly mood. It was then I would dart into the shop before he closed up. Putting my tanner on to the counter, I would ask for my sixpenn'orth of pie bits. Good old Edgar, being jolly and full of good spirit, would chant: "How you going young man?" And, singing away, he would put a large piece of paper on to the counter, slap on a pile of good stewing beef, bang on some sausages and for, good measure, a nice piece of lift.[2]

I would rush home, eager to tell Mum what I'd got. It meant that for my tanner I'd got three good meals. Mum would put the stew into the oven. It was coal-fired and we would fix it to burn slowly all night. Next morning there would be a jar of wonderful stew in delicious, beefy gravy. That, with a bit of good bread, would fill all our bellies.

That made a good start to Sunday, and there was more to come. The lift made us a good dinner and a drop of beef dripping, with enough cold beef left to make us all a good sandwich the next day. And the sausage? That was yet another meal to be enjoyed. Good old Edgar!

# CORRUPT AUTHORITY

It was 1927. I was 12 and had moved up to "The Board School for Boys". It was a boys-only school with three classrooms. Two of them seated about 40 boys each and there was another larger room which could take about 80 boys. There were three teachers. Miss Jolley taught Standard 3 – a lovely teacher whom all the boys adored. Standards 4 and 5 were taken by Gaffer Ward. He was a brute of a man; always wore a black bowler hat and a black suit. He looked more like the old style bailiff than a teacher. He had a notorious reputation for thumping lug-'oles. How many ear drums he busted doesn't bear thinking about. He thumped mine a time or two.

Then we had Gaffer Slack, the Headmaster. He taught Standards 6 and 7. He was a well-built chap and smart with it. He liked to talk about his war-time experiences, and the lads were delighted to get him doing this. They would pull all kinds of stunts to get him at it. That usually meant lessons would be forgotten for the rest of the period. He claimed to have suffered damage to his lungs because of a gas raid, but he could belt out songs louder than Pavarotti.

Christmas was coming and it was our last day at school before breaking up for the holidays. During playtime a number of tables had been set up on trestles at the top end of the big classroom. A huge pile of toys had been arranged on the tables. They had been donated by some charity and were for children of the poor. At the end of playtime the lads were assembled in the big room, buzzing with excitement as they eyed the toys. I was one of the poor – indeed, amongst the poorest. My Dad had recently come home from the Sanatorium. He was ill and couldn't work, so we were still living on the hated parish relief. There were other lads though – Barnet, Howard, Thomas and others – who had fathers in regular work. Some were pit boss men, craftsmen and officials, with permanent jobs and good incomes. Poor sods like me always regarded Barnet and such as being rich. They had holidays at the seaside, were always well dressed, with good leather shoes, a suit with shirt and tie, pullover and a cap. They also had Sunday suits to go to Church or Chapel in. Although they were wormy, sneaky little bastards when out of sight of teachers and parents, they were always clean and well dressed, and their Dads were friends of Gaffer Slack and the local bigwigs. So they were favourite pupils.

There were other lads who never had good clothes, but were reasonably clad. For myself, I never had clothes that were adequate for bad weather. Often I could not go to school because I didn't have enough clothes to wear. I usually had a pair of plimsolls, one pair of stockings, and one pair of trousers, very much patched – fine for today's standards, but hardly fitting in those days. But there were times when I didn't have a full set of these things. I did have a cap, though, and a fountain pen: I won them from one of the rich lads at marbles.

Anyway, there was this big heap of toys. Gaffer Slack came in, gave us some spiel about how lucky we were to have such generous and benevolent people providing the loot to enable toys to be bought for such a worthless lot. I gazed at the toys with wondrous expectancy: lovely clockwork train sets, clockwork cars, building bricks – a truly wonderful selection. I eyed the train sets, trembling in the hope that I would get one. What games I could play along with my home-made toys. But alas, it wasn't to be. One of the favourites, Barnet, got the first train set. Then Thomas, and so it went. The value of the toys fell in descending order as they were distributed to a descending order of less "deserving" brats. It was my first and never-to-be-forgotten experience of corrupt authority. You may have guessed – the moment came when there was just one boy left. And I was that one: the least deserving, because I didn't come to school all the time… now facing a corrupt tribunal. One toy left, one boy for it. All my dreams of owning a toy beyond the buying power of Dad and Mum had gone. I was ready for running as I watched the boys and toys disappear. My hopes, my dreams, smashed. I didn't have to guess what I was going to get: for there it was. Forlorn as I was, I felt my belly burning with anger.

The toy was a flat piece of wood, cut to the shape of a monkey and painted red and brown. I reckon I could have found a way of playing with it – but I was so sickened by the unfairness, all I wanted to do was to fling it away. And that is what I did. When the Gaffer handed me the monkey, along with his patronising verbiage, my impulse was to hurl it back at him, but I turned, saying: "I don't want it" and skimmed it along the class room to the sound of the Gaffer's bawling – "Kenyon!" I ran out of the school and all the way home. Shortly after I got home, Alf Lyndley, my mate, brought me a bag of boiled sweets, and an apple and orange. Miss Jolley had sent them.

# BOOTS

The Christmas toy incident over, I was soon to witness another episode of blatant favouritism, committed by what I was later to call, "a load of twisters." In late February, 1928, a supply of children's boots arrived at the school. Don't know who supplied them, but I think it was summat to do with the West Riding County Council. There wasn't enough to go around all the school, but I reckon about half of the kids got a pair. There were about sixty pairs, piled on a long table in a small room at the end of the big classroom: lovely boots, all nice and shiny with good leather soles and studs in them.

At this time the weather was cold and wet, and my only footwear was the usual plimsolls. Because of the weather, and my plimsolls being leaky, I hadn't been to school for the past fortnight. So, knowing about the free boots, I made it to school – Mum, Dad and me expecting, and praying for, a pair of boots. During the morning selected lads were called into the spare room. They tried the boots for fit and were given a pair. Guess who was called first? Why Barney of course, and the rest of the favoured clan.

I didn't get a pair, nor did some other "undeserving" brats. I went home and cried a bit. It was hard for me to understand why some lads who were already wearing good leather shoes should be given boots when I and other lads who had none were left out. It was the kind of corruption which was to shape my life for evermore. I have never since looked at any kind of authority without believing it to be corrupt in some way. And it is still happening.

The boots were never worn by the favoured few. They drifted to other families by way of a favour and a couple of pints in the local Working Men's Club. Some of the parents protested, but nothing came of it. My Dad was recently home from the sanatorium. Our family income was a food voucher which provided only the barest nourishment.

It's a wonder I learned anything at all. I never sat my eleven plus exam because I was away from school at the time. In spite of this, when I got to school, I was always in the top three, and in the last two years top of the class, especially in arithmetic and composition. Mind you, the lads who did sit the eleven plus didn't get to grammar school either. Grammar school wasn't for bright lads destined to become electricians, joiners and suchlike craftsmen. As for lads of my ilk, it was down the pit and filling coal.

## MY FIRST STRIKE

A week or so after the boots dispute I was sounding off to the lads when Gaffer Ward was doing a bit of earwigging. He heard me accusing the teachers of being a load of twisters. "What's that you said?" Wardy snapped.

"You're a load of twisters, Sir," I answered.

Grabbing me by the hair, he snapped: "Come on!" and dragged me along to the Headmaster, Gaffer Slack. Wardy told him what he had heard me say.

"Is this true?" asked the Gaffer.

"Yes sir, you are a load of twisters. You gave boots to Barney and his mates, and they didn't need boots."

"Less of your cheek," he said, brandishing his cane. "Get to your place, and I'll deal with you later."

"No you won't," I said. "I'm not coming to this school again. It's no good." I walked away, and out of the school.

It was Friday, and I went down to see my old mate Titch. His family had moved to Royston, the nearby village some two and a half miles away. Titch had told me that Royston School was a lot better than Carlton. I decided, therefore, that Royston would be my school. I told my parents that I was starting at Royston School – and what I had said to Gaffer Slack.

"Tha did reit lad. They are a load of twisters, all lot of 'em. But I don't think they'll let you go to Royston," said my Dad. Monday morning came and I went off to Royston. I had arranged for Titch to take me into the school. I called at his home and his mother, a widow and a verbose, brawny kind of woman, looked at me and asked, "What's tha doin' comin' to Royston?" I told her what had gone off, "Aye," she said loudly. "They're a warm lot o buggers, that lot in Carlton. That's why we moved to Royston. But I dunt think they'll have thi in't school here."

Titch took me along to his school and introduced me to the headmaster. He was a kindly sort of bloke and I liked him straight away. He asked me why I wanted to come to his school. I told him the story of the toys and the boots, and added, to strengthen my case (Titch's mother put me up to this) that we might be flitting to Royston, and I thought that I might just as well start at this school now. There was some muttered conversation among the teachers and then the Headmaster turned to me and said: "Yes, you can come to this school now lad, for the time being, anyway."

I was enrolled into a class. It seemed a bit strange at first. The system was different; it seemed easier somehow, and the teachers were friendly. I felt more at ease, and I wanted to try that much harder. I had six happy weeks at that school, and no bother from anyone. Then there was a measles epidemic in Royston and the school was closed for a fortnight. At that time we were having some fine spring weather so I used to go out and watch the lads going off to the Carlton school.

Then things started to happen. Bobby Jones, the school inspector, called to see my Dad and after several visits threatened him with prosecution and all sorts of dire punishments if he did not make me go back to my old school. Bobby Jones was well known to be a swine and a bully boy. Nobody liked or respected him. Dad, much as he hated it, was forced eventually to take me back to school where I had to confront Gaffer Slack and Wardy.

My class had been having lessons about Oliver Cromwell and, because of my exploits, the lads named me "Oliver". The Gaffer snorted contempt at this and scornfully parried, "His name is Joe Kenyon, not Oliver..." Cashy, the big lad of the class, shouted, "They call his Grandad Oliver, so Joey's name can be Oliver."

Gaffer Slack, knowing that I was coming back to the school, had already arranged a warm welcome for me. He had placed a big blackboard in front of the class. On it there was a cartoon drawing of me, hair hanging untidily down each side of my face. Underneath the drawing was written, "This school is not good enough for Kenyon." The class was given a lesson on good behaviour and obedience, and how to get on in the world. At twelve noon, we went out for dinner, the drawing still in place.

At half past one, when we all came back to the classroom, the drawing of Joey Kenyon had been rubbed out, and a wild drawing of the Gaffer had been put on. Underneath it was written: "Gaffer Slack is not good enough for this school." Well, that really blew the lid off. The Gaffer was boiling, full of rage and his face all purple. "Who is responsible for this?" he bawled, swishing his cane. "Don't know, Sir," the lads shouted. "Did you do it?" he yelled at one boy, "You? Or you?" he shouted. Raging like a tiger on the prowl, he moved around the class. "If you don't tell who did this, I shall cane the lot of you." Nobody told, because nobody knew.

Not even me.

The Gaffer kept his promise, brandishing his cane and with no remorse thrashing every lad, once on each hand, as cruelly and as painfully as he could. He left me until last – as usual. By this time he really had worked up a sweat. It was dripping from his chin and nose-end.

"Out in front Kenyon" he bawled. "Put your hand out."

I stuck my hand out and he thrashed me, three times on each hand. What made him more foul-tempered was that some of the lads had nervously withdrawn their hands as the cane came down. If he expected that from me, he was frustrated. I stared at him, arms held rigid. I may have winced a bit, but I never flinched. "Good old Oliver," some of the lads murmured.

# PAWNSHOPS

One of the jobs that earned me a few coppers every week was to walk two and a half miles to the pawnshop in the next village and two and a half miles back again on a Friday afternoon or Saturday morning. I went there to redeem goods which had been pledged on Monday morning. It was usually the old man's best suit. Getting into the pawnshop habit was an entrapment many women fell for. It was the easiest way for the housewife to get a few bob quickly if she was hard up. And once a woman got into the habit, it took some flaming getting out of. Four or five weeks good wages might get her out of it, but good wages were scarce and poor wages were the rule. The best suit could be pawned on the Monday and redeemed for the weekend, so that her man had a suit to go out in. But if the wife used her money to get the suit out on Friday she would be short of brass on the Monday, and so back went the suit.

Monday was always a busy day for pawnbrokers – the day when women took back the things they had taken out for the weekend. It was fun to watch the antics new or rare customers used to get up to before they made their desperate dash to the back door and into the shop. They would stand across the road, and look around to see if anyone was watching for 10 or 15 minutes before they made that mad dash. For newcomers it can be very humiliating, as poverty always is. But the hard cases and the regulars were past that stage. Pawnshop parcels were very distinctive. Coats or suits were wrapped in thick brown paper, then pinned at each end with a couple of thick straight pins known as "pawnshop pins". String was never used; it was too slow. This was why some of the more "respectable" would pay a penny for me to fetch their parcels. Anyone, at any age, could redeem a parcel, which is why I was able to earn a copper. But to pledge an article you had to be 14 years or over. Later, because I had become so well known to the pawnbroker, he allowed me to pledge too, although I was under age.

The loan on a good suit was £1, but after a time its value would fall. One Monday, when I took a suit in, I put it, as usual, on the counter and said, "£1 please." The pawnbroker replied: "Seventeen and six."

"Seventeen and six!" I exclaimed in disgust.

"Aye. Seventeen and six."

"But I got a pound on this last week."

"Aye, you did. But it's wearing out."

"Well you know for a fact I will fetch it back next Friday. Why seventeen and six?"

"Seventeen and six", he grunted.

"Pooh" I said, "You can let me have a bit more than that."

Looking at me, he said, "Seeing as I know you – eighteen and six." And eighteen and six it had to be.

Because I could now pledge, the women that were a bit ashamed of people knowing they were pawning things would call on me at home, late of a Sunday evening, and whisper, "Can you take this in for me Joey? And get what you can out of the old skinflint."

Pawnshop men never took chances. There was no sentiment about their business. The goods that were pledged were always worth many times more than the loan secured. When you pledged, you paid two pence for your card, and a penny interest. When you redeemed, if after only a week, you paid another two pence. If goods were left in longer than a week, the interest would pile up.

They also had a shrewd idea as to what would be a temporary pledge – the old man's suit, for example – and what looked likely to be a longer term pledge. If they were blankets, sheets or boots, they would have to be new or in very good nick. Pawning bedding or other household goods was usually a sign of near desperation and an indication that the more common article, like the suit, was still in hock. If it were a watch, a wedding ring, musical instruments or similar goods, the pawnbroker had a good idea that it was a pledge that was not likely to be redeemed in a hurry. In this case, the loan was kept to a minimum. Sometimes people unable to redeem their goods would sell the pledge card to a third person for a fraction of what it was worth. There were many times when housewives, desperate for a few bob, would buy a bale of bedding or towels on credit; then take them to the pawnshop right away.

When you got into the clutches of the "popshop man" it took a lot of getting out of. There were three brass balls hanging over the shop, and they used to say that meant "It's two to one that owt tha teks in dun't come art again".

# CHRISTMAS 1928

By Christmas 1928 I was thirteen years old and near the end of my schooling. I well remember going out to sing Christmas carols. We used to call it mumming. My first call was at the Young's house. Mr Young was a self-employed joiner and carpenter. The neighbours considered him fairly wealthy because he had regular work and a regular income. He was a polite gentleman, standing about five feet four inches tall. He would have been taller, but his legs were bowed. He lived with a wife and daughter in a better-class terraced house within our neighbourhood.

Where I lived was known as Grayson's Yard which consisted of two rows of terraced houses – eight in each row. To the end of the yard there were two large detached houses. One of these was a general dealer's shop and an off-licence shop. The other was a butcher's shop. Our two rows were separated by middens and open lavatories. There were no WCs. Two or three neighbours had to share a midden and there were often violent disputes as to whose turn it was to clean the midden, especially if it had been allowed to get into a bit of a state. Going to it on a Sunday morning was often a horrible experience – especially if it had been used by someone who liked his booze on a Saturday night.

The Youngs lived in one of the front rows, which were stone built and of a better quality than the back rows which were of red brick. The front-row houses had a larger kitchen, which had a coal-fired open range that kept the kitchen warm, and heated the oven. It was more used as a living room than a kitchen. The front room was used as a parlour and was usually very nicely furnished. Houses in the back row of the yard where we lived had just one room downstairs – the living room – and a small kitchen with one cold water tap and a stone sink in the corner. In another corner there was a coal-fired copper, used mostly for boiling water for the weekly wash or having a bath. There was no pantry, and food was kept either in a small cupboard in the living room, or on a couple of shelves in the coal place which was part of the kitchen.

Later on, Mr Young bought a piece of land and built his own detached house with hot water, a bathroom and all the other luxuries available at that time. Mrs Young was a bonny kind of woman, a bit on the plump size. She spoke quietly and gently and for the most part kept herself to herself. She used to pay one of the neighbours to do her stint at cleaning the midden.

Every Tuesday, a brewer's dray, hauled by two great shire horses, came round delivering barrels of beer and other drinks. Mr Young always had a barrel delivered – I think it held around eight gallons – and two cases of stout. Deliveries were also made to Edgars the Butcher, and to Mrs Bill, the owner of the local fish and chip shop.

I called first at Youngs' to sing my Christmas carol: "Hark the Herald Angels Sing". I had been rehearsing it for weeks. I stood outside the door, as close as I could get. It was one of those damp, cold evenings with a chilly breeze blowing. I didn't have a coat or jacket to wear and I was feeling more than a bit shivery. But I did need the money for Christmas. I had been in Youngs' a few times because I sometimes ran errands for Mrs.Young. So I kept thinking of the warm, cheerful glow there would be in the house. I sang my carol on the door step, wished them all a happy Christmas, and knocked hopefully on the door. Mr Young opened the door and invited me in. There was a lovely big coal fire burning, coloured trimmings hanging from the ceiling and a table laden with Christmas fare. Mrs Young had been baking and there was that wonderful aroma of freshly baked fruit, jam tarts and mince pies and other goodies which make Christmas so wonderful.

"You sing very well Joey," said Mrs Young, as she handed me a cup of hot cocoa and a mince pie. Then she gave me three pence. We talked for a few minutes. I was now feeling warm and glowing inside, and then, as I made to leave, she wrapped up a large piece of Christmas cake she had made and gave it to me.

The next call was at Edgars, the butcher. I sang my carol, knocked at the door, and Edgar appeared – a tall lanky man, always singing and chanting. I could hear some merriment going on and they were obviously celebrating Christmas in proper style. Edgar, half tanked up and singing merrily, "Happy Christmas, young Joey!", gave me a tanner. I thought I had been given the moon, and was beginning to feel half tanked myself. Full of cheer and energy, I now waltzed off to Mrs Bill's. Mrs Bill owned the local fish and chip shop. It was a wooden hut and contained two coal-fired pans along with the usual accoutrements of these shops. She was a jolly, balloon-shaped woman, around five feet tall with a red face and lots of thick black hair, who spoke in a very broad Yorkshire accent. Her jokes when serving at the counter were often more than a bit salty, and the customers loved it.

Every evening, except Sunday, it was one of my little jobs to go up to the fish shop – the "chipoil", as it was known – to collect two empty quart bottles – four pints – and then to walk to the "beer-off" for two quarts of "Old Tom" for Mrs. Bill. Old Tom was a kind of stout brewed by the local brewery, and Mrs Bill loved it. Every now and again, while she was cooking, she would pour out a cupful of her beer, and winking at the customers, she would say "I love a drop of cold strong tea," and down it would go.

I used to sit for a while on a beer crate near one of the fires, and now and again she would say, "Put some coil on't fire Joey lad." Using a small copper shovel, I would stoke up the fires to the right amount to keep the pans at the correct heat for frying. Mrs Bill cooked wonderful fish and chips – much better than the famed Harry Ramsden's. She often boasted that she used only the very best beef dripping. I can vouch for her dripping, because she would wrap up a lump, saying, "Here Joey lad, tek this hooam. It'l put some flesh on thi booerns." It was really gorgeous dripping and I used to cut myself a couple of slices of bread and thicken it with dripping and plenty of salt. Wow, it was delicious! Indeed, I developed such a taste for bread and beef dripping, my dear wife later became aware of this, and when cooking the Sunday roast she always made sure there was a cup of good beef dripping for me. When it was time for tea she would make me a couple of good sandwiches thickened with dripping and I would devour them with gusto.

The chip-oil always had plenty of customers, and trade for Mrs Bill was very good. One of the things I learned about her was that, as she consumed her beloved Old Tom, she became even more jovial and even more generous with her servings of fish and chips. It paid to shop late at Mrs Bills'. After a while, I would say, "I'm going now, Mrs Bill, and she would respond, "Hang on a bot lad." Then, wrapping up a couple of fish and chips, "Here, tek these wi thi lad."

I sang my carol for her and Mrs Bill came to the door. "Come in Joey lad; tha looks half frozen. Get this darn thi." Then, giving me a glass of her home brewed rhubarb wine, she said, "This'll warm thi up." I downed the wine with great relish. It was potent stuff. She poured me another glass, saying, "This'll warm thi cockles up," and then gave me a sixpenny piece, and off I went to my next call. I did five or six more calls where I received a penny or tuppence. Finally, since it was getting on for around ten o'clock, I decided that I would go to the "big house" where the Riddings lived, and then pack it in.

The gates there were open, so I knew that the dogs would be fastened up. As I walked up the drive towards the front doors, I noticed three or four cars parked. One, I believe, was a Bentley, belonging to the son who was at Oxford. As I got to the large double doors, the curtains of one of the large front rooms were open, the room was all lit up and I saw a massive Christmas tree, packed with all kinds of parcels, lights, and tinsel. There was so much noise coming from around two dozen men and women, I told myself, that lot are never going to hear me singing from here. So I gave two great pulls at the bell rope, and then, as I saw someone approaching, I began to sing as lustily as I could. The door opened and old pompous Riddings himself appeared – all rotund and jolly, and no doubt full of good Christmas glut and guzzle. "Come in young man," he said, "we can't hear you sing out here." I followed Pompous into a very large room which looked big enough to play football in. There were carpets on the floor, lots of fine furniture and chairs scattered around, and in one corner a grand piano at which a young woman was sitting. A noisy crowd of people, sitting around or standing, glass in hand, were eyeing me up and down as though I was something the cat dragged in. I didn't feel comfy at all; just amazed at so much ostentatious luxury. Then old Riddings called for quiet, saying "This young man is going to sing a Christmas carol for us."

I didn't like the look of the people – stuck up, I thought – but I pulled myself together, sang my carol and wished them all a Merry Christmas. Pompous took hold of a glass, dropped a few coppers into it, and passed the glass around. I had just learned my first lesson about "class" and hated the thought that I had been made to sing for my supper. Didn't know it at the time, but later I thought they had seen me as a pathetic figure of fun. And this was shown in their response. Pompous retrieved the glass, handed it to me as though he had given me the world. I emptied it and counted 18 pennies. From thirty people. Skinny sods, I thought, as I walked away from the house. But I soon cheered up. I had had a good night.

I now had to get to the beer-off, before it closed at half past ten. This was a mixed sort of shop, fairly large and with three counters around an open-ended rectangle. One side was for sweets, fruit, and general groceries. Another, opposite, was for various household goods: pans, brushes, small items of clothing and a variety of knick-knacks. Facing you, as you walked into the shop, was the beer counter. It had three beer pumps, bitter, Old Tom and mild. On the shelves behind were bottles of beer, stout and pop, cigs and other things. The shop had two large windows and, between them, a double door. One door was bolted on the inside, the other was free to be opened. A catch at the top of the door struck a large bell as you entered.

On getting to the shop, I first looked into the windows to get some ideas of what I might buy as presents for my family – my Mum, Dad, my two younger brothers and two sisters. In one window there were bottles of sweets, toffees, bars of chocolate, and a variety of fruits. The other window had small items of clothing and other household goods. When I saw a fancy bottle of perfume I knew at once I was going to buy it for Mum. I went into the shop and was greeted by Mr. and Mrs Broadhead, the shopkeepers. "Hello Joey," he said, "What can I get you?"

"How much is that bottle of perfume in the window?"

Mrs Broadhead went to the window, took out the bottle, and said, "It is lovely perfume Joey; do you want it for your Mum?"

"Yes. How much is it?"

"Well it's eightpence, but you can have it for sixpence. Your Mum will love this. I've got some."

"I'll take it then, and can I have two fourpenny packets of ten Woodbines for my Dad?"

Mr B reached for the cigs and gave them to me, saying: "Is that it?"

"No, I want some more presents yet." And I asked for five bars of Fry's chocolate – tuppence a packet. They had faces of boys on them.

"And can I have seven oranges and seven red apples?"

Then I saw in a box on the counter a variety of pins and brooches. Choosing a brooch for my Mum, I bought it for sixpence. Then I asked for a packet each of red, blue, green and yellow tissue paper, and two packets of red crepe paper. "I'm going to put some trimmings up when I get home. And can I have a bottle to buy a pint of bitter for my Dad?" Mr Broadhead reached for a clean bottle, filled it with a pint of bitter and put in a cork. They always had a box of fresh corks under the counter. He then took up a red and white sticky label, about six inches long, with a picture of a seal in the middle. He put this over the cork and stuck the rest of the label down the neck of the bottle each side.

"There you are," said Mr Broadhead. "I'm sure your dad will enjoy that." And I reckon there was a bit more than a pint, because the bottle was filled up to the cork. They had some funny laws about alcohol in those days. It was illegal to sell a half pint of beer to anyone under the age of 14, but legal to sell them a pint of beer, provided it was in a bottle and had a seal on the cork.

I now had seven pence left. Showing Mrs Broadhead my pennies, I asked if she could swap them for seven new pennies – new pennies were always issued at Christmas time, and a new penny was always part of the Christmas present, and was meant to bring good luck. A new penny was all that many kids got, and if they were lucky an apple or an orange as well.

Mr Broadhead reached for a brown paper carrier bag, and put all my presents safely inside. "You'll be able to carry them a lot easier now, Joey," he said, as he handed the bag to me. I made to leave the shop, and as I got to the door Mrs Broadhead called me back. Then I watched as Mr Broadhead emptied boiled sweets from a jar into a paper bag – a good pound of them. Handing them to me, he said, "Take these with you, and a Happy Christmas, Joey," and Mrs Broadhead gave me a little peck on the cheek and walked me to the door.

I hurried home, full of joy because I had got presents for all the family. As I walked into the house, my Dad greeted me and said: "You're a bit late lad, I was becoming a-worried for you."

"I've been carol singing and I've bought some presents from Broadheads." I then emptied the contents of my bag on to the table. Picking up the perfume and the brooch, I handed it to Mum and said, a bit elated, "These are for you Mum. Do you like them?"

My Mum opened the perfume and, smelling it, exclaimed: "Oh it's lovely lad." And giving me a kiss, she went on, "You shouldn't have spent your bit of money, lad; but they're very nice, and thank you."

"You're a grand lad," said my Dad, and put his arm around my shoulder.

Then, all excited, I said, "Look what I've got for our Selina, and our Jack, Helen and Jim".

I showed them the chocolate, apples and oranges, and the new pennies. Handing some of them over to Mum and Dad: "These are for you as well."

My Dad was looking at the tissue paper. "I'll make you some trimmings then, lad."

My Mum then made me a cup of tea and cut me a thick slice of Christmas cake she had baked a week or two earlier, but had kept for a surprise. She also gave me a fresh-baked mince pie. Mm, I really felt happy, it was all so lovely.

Then we all sat around the table – the kids were in bed – making Christmas trimmings. My Dad was good at making trimmings. He knew several ways of cutting the paper to make different-style trimmings. My Mum was handy too. She used the crepe paper to make beautiful shawls to drape around the mirror over the mantelpiece, and around three large framed pictures we had on the wall.

I went up to bed. I shared a bed with my two younger brothers. They were fast asleep, and, although I was dying to tell them what I had got for them, I eased myself into bed as quietly and gently as I could.

Come the morning, the kids were up bright and early, and Jimmy asked:

"I wonder if Santa's been?"

"Why don't you go down and see?" My Mum and Dad had laid my presents for them in front of the hearth. So down they went, and I quickly dressed and followed them. "He's been, he's been," they excitedly chanted. And very much to their surprise and joy, they saw their stockings and presents laid out for them. By now, Selina and Helen had joined us. It was really Christmas!

In addition to the bits I had bought them, Jimmy, aged 3, had a set of building bricks – wooden cubes, and on each side of them there was a picture, or part of a picture, so by matching them together you could form six different pictures of a landscape, or a famous building. Jack, aged 8, had a small train set. It had a track about 12 inches in diameter, with a clockwork engine, tender, and coach. He was really happy, winding up the engine and watching it whizz round. Helen, aged 6, had a pretty doll with flaxen hair, eyelids that drooped when it was laid down, and some clothes which Mum had made for it. Selina, who was 11, also got a doll, a bit larger than Helen's and Mum had made clothes for that as well.

And for Joey? What a surprise! There was a large box of paints, two paintbrushes, some mixing bowls and a large picture book, with pictures ready for painting. They couldn't have chosen anything more delightful for me. I have always had a passion for drawing and painting, but what paints I did manage to get now and then were what I had won from the other lads.

By this time, Mum and Dad were up. Dad got a nice fire going and Mum was cooking breakfast for us all. An egg, some bacon, fried bread and some toast. What with all the presents, a nice cosy fire and all the trimmings and decorations, everything about the house was really wonderful.

The reason all this happiness could be created was because my Dad, for some weeks, had been able to do a number of odd jobs and earn a few shillings each week. Some of this had been set aside for Christmas. Meanwhile my Mum had saved up at the butchers enough to buy a piece of pork and some other goodies for dinner. She was a good cook when she had the chance. With the pork and other delights she had prepared, we had a wonderful Christmas dinner and finished it off with some Christmas pudding Mum had made, smothered with hot, delicious, home-made custard.

We talked and sang, had lots of fun around the table, and Mum and Dad looked so happy. They had done us proud. It was a truly, truly, happy Christmas. Especially for me!

# II IN AND OUT OF THE PIT

# THE RIGHT TO SIT

The end of July meant the break-up of school for the long summer holidays. But for me it was the end of school days and my entry into the world of work. I was 14 and looking forward to my first job. For a boy like me, living in a pit village, most of the jobs available were in the three collieries nearby. There were two in the village where I lived, and another at Royston, the next village.

From the day I left school I did the daily rounds, regularly visiting all three pits: the two Woodmore Pits near my home and the Monckton Pit at Royston, 3 miles away. There wasn't much joy in it though. Every day I walked to the pit, waited in a kale (a queue) where other men were waiting for the pit undermanager to come out of the pit, usually at 2 p.m. He would enter his office and then after a wait of ten minutes or so, the first man would be called in. Eventually, after a long wait, I would reach the office door, knock and walk in, and blurt out "Have you any jobs?" Most often I would be standing before Jim Ward, an undermanager in the nearest pit to my home: a big, brawny, clever sod. He would give me a long look, notice my small size, then say gruffly, " not today."

I was desperate for a job because I knew the few shillings a week would be a godsend to my Mum. There was always a long queue of men, shuffling towards the office door, cap in hand. Many times I would try to sort out in my mind the best approach. I had the feeling that somehow there had to be a better way of asking for a job, but I never could work it out. Sometimes there was a gleam of hope, especially when I saw men leaving the office with that magical chit of paper in their hand and trotting off across the pit yard to the time office. I knew that on those days they were "setting on". But alas, for me it was always that gruff "not today". After six weeks of trying, my Mum, being desperate for the few shillings a job would bring and knowing how keen I was to become a wage earner, wrote a letter and told me to take it to the pit manager. The manager looked at me. "You're not very big lad, are you?" he remarked. Then he reached for a chit – the signing-on chit – signed it and said, "take this to Lewis Jackson." He was the boss at the time office. "He'll sign you on, and start work in the morning in the Haighmoor Seam."

Away I galloped, across the pit yard and up the steps to Jackson's office. Jackson took my chit and, sniffing, looked me up and down. He was a stuffy, pompous bloke, a toad to the manager, but arrogant and contemptuous to the workmen. He wrote down my name, address etc., and then asked me to sign a couple of forms. Looking at the form he remarked, almost friendly, "Your handwriting is very neat. I'm surprised you want to go down the pit". Then he gave me an authority to sign at the lamp room for a pit lamp. At the lamp room, they gave me a metal identity disc, number 672, and told me to call for a lamp next morning. I couldn't get home quick enough.

"I've got a job! Start in the morning!" I sang with joy. The next thing for Mum to do was to get me fixed up with some pit rags. Mrs Nicholson from next door came in and Mum told her the good news.

"I'll want some clogs Mum," I said.

"Don't worry about that," Mrs N said. "'Lijah will make you a pair". 'Lijah was her husband, the disabled cobbler. She also gave me an old jacket. It was a bit big for me, so Mum cut it down to size. It felt champion; the first jacket I had ever worn. I didn't have any trousers either, but Mum got me a pair of shorts from Uncle Tom. It was a bit embarrassing wearing shorts, but after a few weeks Mum found me a pair of long'uns. I only had the one shirt, so Mum had to wash and iron it after every shift, so that I had a clean one to go out in. She got me a new shirt after my first pay day.

Come 5am next morning, I set off eagerly for my first shift down the pit. Went to the lamp room window, shouted "672!" and got myself an oil lamp. They didn't have electric lamps those days. Then I had to find my way down the pit. I approached a bloke blowing at his lamp to try it for safety, and I asked him how I got to the Haighmoor seam.

"Follow me," he said.

We crossed the pit yard, went up about 20 steps to the shaft head, then we pulled hard – very hard – at a ventilation door. It was thick and very heavy, with a second door 3 yards beyond. These doors stopped air from short-circuiting to the shaft and blocking the ventilation system. Below the shaft mouth there was a massive fan, 10 feet in diameter. It was rotating at a terrific speed with a noise like a thousand banshees, sucking air from the down-cast shaft through all the workings and airways of the pit, through the ventilating doors, and back to the surface up the upcast shaft. Because of the force of the air being sucked round the pit, there was always a howling, whistling hiss of air trying to escape through the doors. It was a bit scary at first, but one got used to it.

Then I walked towards the "chair" – a lift like a cage, with two decks taking ten men in each. Before stepping into it, I gave my identity disc to the banksman – the man responsible for signalling the chair down the shaft. Giving the disc to him was a way of recording each man who went down the pit.

Down the shaft we dropped; it seemed we had gone into free-fall, my stomach got fast in my throat and I thought my ears were going to burst. I tried peering through the slots of the chair, but the flicker of my oil lamp and the speed of the chair stopped me from seeing properly. All I could make out was the flash of the shaft girders as we whistled past them. Scary, but very exciting. Then the stale smell of air that had circulated through the pit hit my nose. All the smells and stinks of the pit were in it: the kind of rare perfume you always get in an upcast shaft. Then, to my amazement, as I stepped from the chair, I saw the pit bottom, all lit up with electric lights. It was high and wide, with brick whitewashed walls surrounding it. I really didn't know what I was expecting to see. I just stood and looked around this strange new world. Then I woke up and saw the men walking to their respective departure points for their places of work.

"I've just started this morning," I said to a passing bloke; "Where do I go?"

"If you walk up there lad, about forty yards, and turn to the left; just down there on your left, you will see the box-office". (A sort of bricked office for the use of the undermanager and deputies). "Go in there and ask for Mr Ward".

I found my way to the box-office and asked for Mr Ward. He saw me and turned to a deputy saying, "He's going door trapping on the north level. Tell the corporal to take him there."

The corporal, a big heavyweight bully-boy type, was ostensibly employed for his strength to lift coal tubs back on the track, but in reality to thump the pony drivers if they got out of line. He walked me up the level for about 500 yards and stopped at a heavy wooden door, put there to control the ventilation.

"Tha keeps this door shut, all the time. Tha never leaves it open, dust 'ear?" snapped the corporal. "When the ponies come with the tubs, let 'em through, then shut door again." Then off he went, into the darkness. Holding my lamp up, I looked around in its dim glow. The roof and walls of the roadway in which I stood were of solid sandstone rock and didn't need supports. I didn't know of this, and I wondered how it was all holding up. The dim glow of the lamp, the surrounding darkness, and the ghostly hum and whistle of the air escaping through the door – it all felt like the gateway to hell. I opened the door nervously, looked through ..... nothing there but a silent blackness. Slamming the door shut, I did a sort of mouselike exploration. I moved cautiously from the door, holding my lamp out, to see better. There wasn't much to see really. Just the rock of the roof and sides and the blackness beyond.

Then I thought I would sit down, but there was nothing to sit on except a flat piece of stone. By the looks of it, the previous door-trappers had sat there; the stone was clean and a bit shiny. At the front there was a mound of dried hard rust, caused by the frequent spitting of tobacco juice by the door-trapper.

I wasn't happy with this arrangement. They used to say that if you sit on cold stone you'll get piles. So I decided I needed something to sit on. After a few shifts and feeling more confident, I looked for materials I could use to make a seat. From time to time there would be rolls of brattice cloth in passing tubs.[3] I nicked a roll of brattice and eight sleepers, and set about making me a comfortable seat. I fastened four sleepers together to form the base of the seat, and then fixed the other sleepers to form a gently sloping back-rest. Then I nailed four sheets of brattice onto the sleepers. By hanging my lamp on a jutting stone, just above my head and behind me, I could sit back, feeling nice and cosy.

I fastened a length of rope to the door handle, ran it to a nail in the wall beside me; then, when the tubs came, I pulled the door open with the rope, and when they had passed I would kick the door back. That way, I could settle down and read a book. Then one morning, being so engrossed with my reading, I failed to notice old Wardie – the undermanager – creeping up on me, until he bawled out, "What the fucking hell do you think you are up to? And who told you to build that fucking settee?"

Startled, I jumped up and saw him coming at me, stick raised. He's going to clobber me, I thought, and so I lunged forward, head first, right into his guts. He went sprawling onto the ground, breaking his stick and knocking his lamp out. He got up, calling me all the pit names he could think of.

"You fucking little bastard, I'll bleeding sack you for this! Where's your fucking lamp?" Taking my lamp from the wall, he bounced through the door, still cursing me from here to hell. So there I was, in complete blackness, totally blind. I crawled around the floor, found the door, then the rope, and felt my way back to my seat.

"I've had it now," I thought. "Bugger 'im, he asked for it." Then I sat there in the dark, listening to the hum of the air escaping around the edges of the door. After what seemed an age, the door banged open, and the corporal appeared, cursing and sounding off. "I've brought your lamp back, and Wardie has told me to knock down that fucking settee tha's built."

"Tha's not bloody touching it!" I shouted. Then, as he made for me, threatening me with every kind of obscenity, I grabbed a stone and stood guard. Bang! He rushed at me and fisted me in the mouth, splitting my lip. And Crack! I felt his shin go as I toe-ended him with my clog. He dropped down on his knees, hugging and rubbing his damaged shinbone. "You lousy, rotten, fucking little bastard! I'll bleeding string thi up, when I get my hands on thi," he groaned.

"Thee try it mate, and tha'll get this," I replied, brandishing the stone in my hand. He got up and, limping and cursing, tried to come at me again. Wham! I let fly with the stone. It hit him, and he yelled and bawled his foul language . So – Wallop! I let him have another one. My blood was up and, feeling more cocky, "Thee try it again," I called, "and I'll knock ten different kinds of shit outer thee."

He hobbled away, spitting and mouthing all kinds of threats. Came the end of the shift, I went out of the pit, and as I put my lamp in, the lamp man shouted; "Kenyon! Wilford wants to see thee. Tha's to go up to his office now."

Walking across the pit yard and being aware of my split lip, I rubbed at it with my thumb to open it up again. Standing in the office, in front of the managers' desk – Mr Wilford behind it – I pushed at my lip with my tongue so as to make it bleed again.

Eyeing me up and down, Wilford said, "Take your cap off lad." Then he went on, "It looks like you are in trouble young man. Mr Ward has accused you of assaulting him. You knocked him down to the floor, hurt his ribs, broke his stick and knocked his lamp out."

"Well" I said, "He came charging at me with his stick and he was going to hit me with it, just because I was sitting down, and I'm not going to stand there all day, at side o' the door".

Wilford interrupted. "He didn't hit you though, did he?"

"No, but he would have done if I hadn't stopped him. All I did was butt him with my head, and he fell down. I didn't break his stick and I didn't knock his lamp out. He did it because he fell down."

"Now then young man, you're getting a bit too cheeky." And then, in a cool deliberate style, he spelled out slowly, adding emphasis on every word, "You have committed a very serious offence. Not only have you

assaulted Mr Ward, you also stole some sleepers and a roll of brattice."
"I didn't steal 'em. They're still down 'pit. I only used them to sit on."
Wilford interrupted, "You also assaulted the corporal, causing serious damage to his shin bone. He had to have treatment in the ambulance room. You also threw stones at him, which could have caused even more serious damage. These are all very, very serious and dangerous offences, especially when committed underground. You can be fined – even sent to prison – for these offences."

"Well, the corporal hit me first. He fisted me," and, touching my split lip, I said, "He did this to me. He assaulted me, so if you're going to summons me, you should summons him as well".

"Alright," Mr Wilford said quietly. "I could sack you, but I know that your mother needs your wages, and so I am going to let you off this time. So off you go." And, as I turned to leave the office, Wilford said: "And that settee will have to come down."

Next morning, when I got to work, the settee was still there, and was never taken down until the level was ripped out and widened for an endless rope and automatic doors to be installed.

The sequel to this story comes one Saturday noon, sixteen years later, in July 1945. I was on my way to town for a couple of jars with the lads and to do a bit of shopping for my lovely wife. I called first at the local pub, where the bus terminates, for a pint of the best. As the landlord pulled my pint, a voice from behind me said "I'll pay for that!"
I looked around and saw Sam Biddle, the one-time agent for Sir William Sutherland's pits, now retired. "Young Kenyon, isn't it?" Biddle asked. "Aye" I said, and "Cheers," as I lifted my glass.

Then Biddle began the story, to the Landlord, about the settee and my being hauled to see the manager. It turned out that he had been sitting in the next office, behind the door, unseen by me, and had heard everything. Then, bursting out laughing, he said "There was young Kenyon, no more than four feet six tall, and not much above four stone in weight wet through, and he was being accused of assaulting Jim Ward, the undermanager, who stood about five feet ten and weighed no less than 15, maybe 16, stone. I was rocking in my chair, nearly pissed myself, as young Kenyon here gave Wilford, the manager, as good as he got. And when young Joe left the office, I said to Wilford, 'He's a spunky little bugger isn't he? Let him keep his settee."

And there hangs a tale, from which, for me and future door trappers, a right was won – the Right to Sit.

# GROWING AND LEARNING

My first wage, for five days door-trapping underground, was four shillings and seven pence. There was a penny "stoppages" which left me with 4/6 to take home. Not much, but a boon to my Mum. It was a happy day for me to be able to give her the money I had earned. From now on, there was a little left over each week to buy clothes or bits of things for the house. There was always something to put on the bread and sometimes to put between the slices. A bit of corned beef, or some cheese, or good old beef dripping. We had meat for Sunday dinner, and sometimes a sweet for Sunday tea. Pineapple chunks, with a bit of tinned cream was the favourite. Sometimes my Mum would buy a couple of large jaffa oranges, slice them, and share them out to the family. On a Sunday we had a fried egg, sometimes with a bit of bacon and fried bread when we were rich. There was also the odd tanner to pay weekly towards buying blankets and sheets for the beds, with coloured coconut matting to put on the floor. We always had a penny for the gas and didn't have to read by candlelight or by the light of the fire.

The deputy, who had a great liking for me and knew that I needed every penny I earned, would sometimes find work for me on Saturday morning or Saturday night if a special job was being done. While I was still fourteen I got a pay rise, and one every six months after that until I was sixteen, and then I got a whopping pay rise of a shilling a shift. The reason for the big pay rise was because I had reached the age when I had to get an insurance card and pay a stoppage for sickness and insurance cover. It was private insurance and we could choose our own insurance company. I was in the Pru. If you had to go on sick, you got a sick note from your Doctor, which was free because miners had a pay stoppage at work which covered us for all medical and hospital treatment. You handed your sick note to the insurance collector who would then pay you the following week.

When I got my first pay packet, Mum gave me sixpence pocket money, which gradually increased as my wages went up. On my first Saturday, with sixpence burning a hole in my pocket, I went into Barnsley to look around the shops. It was three miles to Barnsley, and the bus fare was tuppence each way. That was a bit too much for me. I would have hardly owt left if I went on the bus, so I walked it both ways. On my first outing I roamed about the town, looking in the shops. Then I got lost, and found myself looking into a scruffy second-hand bookshop. All my life I had wanted to own a book. And when I saw all the wonderful books – books of all sizes, some on shelves, some piled on the counter and around the shop floor, many of them covered in dust – I looked at them wistfully. Some were bound in leather, green, red and yellow. There were books about subjects I'd never heard of before. After a long look, I checked the money in my pocket and bought a great big leather-bound dictionary for tuppence. I thought it would help me to understand words all the better. Unfortunately the book disappeared during the war.

Shortly after buying the dictionary I bought another book, leather-bound and padlocked. It was 'The Pilgrim's Progress and Other Works' of John Bunyan, with a preface and memoir of the author. Luckily this survived the war and is still one of my prized possessions. I bought many other books on every subject you could think of. I was anxious to learn and, although I could hardly understand a word they said, I read them avidly from cover to cover.

My subjects were economics, philosophy, psychology, logic, anatomy, physiology – every subject you could think of. The Authors were Ruskin, Bacon, Plato, Aristotle, Wells, More and many others. Indeed, when I was caught and reproved for reading down the pit as a door-trapper in 1929, it was one of Ruskin's books that I was reading. I ploughed through them, eager to learn, but without any real understanding – all haphazard and without any guidance. But somehow some of it sunk in, and I became quite a formidable talker and debater amongst my mates. Many a time, when a group of us were sat in the pit yard, having 'five' before we went down the pit on the afternoon shift, the agent and manager as they walked past us would say "I see you have the chair again Joe."

Even though I had to struggle many hours trying to understand what I was reading, especially the books on logic, it all served me in good stead years later when I became involved in negotiations with management, especially during a dispute. It allowed me to quickly spot a falsehood within the propositions the management put forward and to exploit this to my own advantage. Some of the union officials didn't like this, especially if they had sent a dud down to negotiate for us. I remember one occasion when we were on strike for an increase in wages and a review of our contract – at this time each pit or group of fillers in a particular seam, negotiated their own contracts and rates of pay, and we were on strike for a pay increase and a change in our contract. The Union had sent down a member of the executive to negotiate for us. This chap, an absolute twit, had been chosen, not because of his negotiating skills, but just because he was a member of the Yorkshire Area Executive and it was his turn. Some of the lads from the executive were good at their jobs – committed and keen to do their best – but some, like the mugwump we got, were hopeless. Wise management will always recognise that it is better to have keen, militant negotiators than easy-goers. That way, grievances won't fester and strikes are avoided.

Anyway, we had a right banana. He thought he was a socialist, even militant. In reality he was devious, a bit of a crackpot and full of self-importance. Several times I had to shut him up, or we would have finished up with a strike or go-slow. After some bantering the Coal Board Official made an offer – a minimal offer – and our pompous friend jumped up, shouting "I accept." For him, any offer was a victory which he could take back to the union saying he had won an increase. I smartly put him right. "Tha'll accept nowt a't sort" And then, turning to the management, I said, "It's not for him to accept or ME to accept. It's for the lads to accept and I can tell you now, I don't accept it, and neither will they. If you want to get us back to work, you'll have to 'up' your offer." The manager called me a blackmailer. "No," I said, "I'm your friend, and I'm just giving you some friendly advice. If I was wanting the strike to go on, as you say I am, I would accept that offer, and take it back to the lads, and I know where they would tell me to stuff it."

The meeting then resumed, and our friend from the exec never spoke again. Finally we reached a settlement, getting all that we had asked for – a change in the terms of our contract, and a few more coppers in the pay tin.

But to get back to my early membership of the toiling class. It was early summer 1931. Some of the lads had gotten bikes, but they were mostly heavy, sit-up-and-beg machines, bought for them by their parents. The two most favoured bikes were the Raleigh and the BSA – made by Birmingham Small Arms. It was known locally as the 'bloody sore arse', but they were good, bonny bikes.

In my school days only the rich kids had bikes. But now lots of lads were getting them. All you had to do was to walk into a shop of the main dealers, pay two bob deposit, promise to pay a bob a week for a year and ride away. My dad was at home at this time and I was approaching my sixteenth birthday when I would get the big pay rise. So I asked him if I could buy a bike, and he said, "Of course lad," and gave me a couple of bob for the deposit. I breezed into town and, after some inspection, plumped for a BSA racing model. It was a lovely bright blue colour, not black like the other bikes, with shiny chrome wheels and adjustable drop handlebars. It was beautiful, light and speedy. It certainly made me the envy of the other lads, and I was always glad to let them have a spin on it. Soon they were getting them too.

I was pally at this time with Joe Lowe, my workmate at the pit. He lived in Grimethorpe, where his step-dad, Ernie Spooner, worked as a coal cutter. Now that I had a bike I was able to ride over to "Grimy" and knock around with him. He fancied himself as a boxer, so we used to go for sparring sessions together in the gym. It was a four mile ride to Grimethorpe, mostly across fields with a good cinder track. There was one stretch where I would get my head down and have a really good sprint. What a thrill!

I got into the habit of going to Joe's home to talk with his step-dad, Ernie, who took an interest in me because of my reading. Ernie was an avid reader of all kinds of books to do with human behaviour and understanding. He believed in socialism and taught me a lot about it. He could explain the ideas and writings of Plato, Aristotle, Hume, Kant, Hegel, Locke, Ruskin, Bacon, J S Mill and many others. And when it started in 1936 he joined me as a member of the Left Book Club. We remained firm friends and enjoyed many long talks together until he died of pneumoconiosis in 1966.

Although there was still some unemployment around and wages didn't seem to go up all that much, work was more regular, and somehow things seemed to get a lot better. Instead of the hard grind of struggling to feed the family from one Saturday to the next, there was money available to buy other things as well: better and cleaner hearth rugs, even carpets to cover the floors, and later on the vacuum cleaner instead of the old, down-on-your-knees, brushing and shaking job. There was new furniture – three-piece suites, what a luxury they were! – more comfortable and more hygienic mattresses for the beds in place of the old flea-ridden straw ones. Washing machines eventually, instead of all that bending, scrubbing and dollying. And then we had the gramophone, and later the wireless – everybody had to have a wireless – and then the radiogram, with Ambrose, Henry Hall and other popular dance bands, and – my favourites – the Wurlitzers and brass bands.

Men were getting softer. In place of the old cut-throat the safety razor appeared, and then a blade that would last a whole week instead of just the one shave. Saturday morning was once the shave day but now they were shaving during the week as well. And, by George, they stopped using soap and bought fancy shaving creams, even brushless shaving creams and aftershave – all perfumed and sweet smelling. And tasty, minty, MacLean's toothpaste. On top of all that, men started to walk out dressed in light grey gabardines, pastel coloured shirts, and without wearing a jacket.

At that time it was compulsory to wear a jacket if you went into the working men's club. I remember one sunny Sunday afternoon in 1939 I went into the club, wearing a sort of pastel grey-green pair of slacks, a short sleeved yellow shirt and without a jacket on. The bar steward promptly ordered his staff not to serve me, because I was improperly dressed. The club rule was that if a member took his jacket off he put himself into a fighting mood, and therefore must be barred from the club. Don't know how the committees would take it these days, when the lads walk into the club without jackets and nearly everything else as well. I reckon a young maiden wearing her mini would never have been allowed near the doors, let alone into the club those days. We were seeing the beginnings of what we now call the consumer society.

How long can it go on before our Mother Earth strikes back and nature becomes its own saviour and leveller?

# FIRST LETTER

I was just 14 when I first started to write letters for neighbours needing help or advice. I don't know how I managed it at that age but somehow I did, and I found that it worked. My first letter was to the Clerk of the Parish Council, a Mr Pratt. He was also the Clerk to other Parish Councils around the area.

I was at home one evening, doing a bit of drawing and scribbling which, apart from my time in the gym, was my favourite pastime. There was a knock at the door. Mum answered and I heard a voice ask, "Is your Joey in?" "Yes," said Mum, "Come in." Then she said to me, "Joey, Mrs Evens wants to see you."

I knew Mrs Evens. I remembered going to a concert in the local Church Hall where Jean Evens sang a couple of songs. She was a beautiful singer, bonny looking, and I reckon I had a bit of a school-kid crush for her. Putting a chair beside the table, I asked her to sit down and tell me what her problem was.

"I've come to see if you can write a letter for me, to the Council". "Why, what's wrong?" I asked.

"Well, as you know, I have two children, our Jane is 3 and Tom is 18 months, and I think I am expecting another. I had our Jane to another man before I was married, but his mother wouldn't let him marry me. And then I met Judd and I married him. We've been married now for just over two years. And in all that time, we haven't been able to get a house at all. We have lived in five different sets of lodgings, and each time we have been kicked out because of Judd's violence, especially when he has had a bit too much to drink. Well, this chap we are lodging with now has tried it on with me a couple of times, and when Judd got to know he belted him. Now we've got to get out, and we have nowhere to go. Ever since we got married, we have lived in lodgings and I'm fed up with trying to get a house. In every case we have had to get out because of Judd being too handy with his fist. I've been to see two Councillors, but they don't want to know. They say that Judd is a bother-causer. I keep putting in for a council house, but they keep refusing us."

At this time the whole family were lodging in one room in a small two bedroomed terraced house. One bedroom, the larger one, was just about big enough to hold two double-sized beds if they were skilfully placed. This was used by the family they lodged with, Mr and Mrs Thomas, who had three children, all aged under seven. Their three kids slept in one bed, and the parents in the other. Jean and Judd slept in the smaller room along with their kids, all in the same bed. There was no space for bedroom furniture, even if they had any. Coats and jackets were hung on nails knocked in the wall or the bedroom door. What other few bits and pieces they had were in a box at the foot of the bed.

Downstairs there was a living room, not much more than ten feet by eleven, if that. It was just about big enough to hold a sideboard, table, sofa and a few kitchen chairs. The floors were mostly uncovered, but there was a peggy rug in front of the fire. There were no armchairs – most people didn't have armchairs at that time – and because there were not enough chairs to go round the table the kids had to stand at the table at meal times. The funny thing is, we never saw this kind of thing as a hardship, just as a fact of life.

The kitchen was even smaller, not much bigger than a rabbit hutch, with a bare concrete floor. There was just the one cold water tap and a shallow stone sink. Every morning they went through the routine of putting salt on the snails in the kitchen that were a bit late getting back to their hidey-holes. A similar routine was carried out by crunching boots on the "black clocks" – cockroaches – when they came in at night and put the light on. The living room was similarly infested around the warm fireplace with silver fish. But folks were used to living with these things. The only real solution was to knock the bloody hovels down, but they brought in good rent and could always be let. With four adults and five kids crammed into this house, is it any wonder that they got on each other's nerves?

Jean Evens was a house-proud lass. All she wanted was a home of her own which she could keep nice and clean. She tried to do the best she could, even in lodgings, but it didn't always suit. After moving in to her present digs, because of the scruffiness of the place she went round with a bucket of hot water and a scrubbing brush. She scrubbed out the bare wooden bedroom floor, and the bug-infested walls. She painted the bedsteads with creosote to keep the bugs out of her beds. And then she started on the bare wooden staircase, and that was a scrub too far because Mrs Thomas, the woman she lodged with, picked a fight, suggesting that she was accusing them of being dirty with all her washing and scrubbing. It was doomed from the start to be a short-stay lodging.

Mrs Evens didn't know where to turn. She was never going to settle in that place, and although she pleaded with the Council to give her a house, they wouldn't listen. Jean then went to see two of her local Councillors, told them about her desperate situation and how it was making her and the children ill. But her pleas fell on stony ground; they just were not interested. Indeed, they were callous: one of them told her, "I can't see you getting a house. Your husband is too much of a bother-causer." Well maybe he was, but there were justifiable reasons for him to be so, and that wasn't sufficient reason for Jean to be denied a home of her own.

The real reasons were that the new council houses, built in 1927, were at that time very desirable properties. Most of the houses in the village were in privately rented rows. Some were stone built and were reasonable houses; others, like the sort where Jean lodged, were brick built and much older. Some belonged to private landlords, others to the Colliery. But in almost all of them there was just the one cold water tap in the kitchen, no hot water and no bathroom.

The toilets – "shit-'oles" as they were called – were the open midden type: a small brick room with wooden platforms and two holes where the deposit could be made. They used to stink rotten, especially on Sunday morning. It was worth a Victoria Cross any time to sit in there for longer than a couple of minutes. To make things more memorable, they were shared toilets – two families to one shit-'ole. And that often caused bother, if one or the other family were a bit slow in taking their turn to clean the place. Because of their stench they were built 20 yards away from the houses. Going to the toilet in those days meant a twenty-yard dash across the yard. Quite an ordeal if it was raining, and bloody cold in the winter. Even the pit deputies' houses, although they were better built stone houses, still only had the one cold water tap and middens.

With these standards, the semi-detached council houses were naturally in great demand, even among those who already had houses. They had hot and cold water taps in a well designed kitchen, with a pantry for food; a bathroom – what a boon that was – and, to crown it all, each house had its own water closet, just beside the back door and sheltered. Competition for a tenancy was rife. Lots of people who already had houses – many of them pit deputies who could offer a reward – got a tenancy almost on demand. It was also noted that friends and relations of councillors got houses, even though they were not in need. But not poor Jean. Her pocket was empty. And then Jean told me about one glaring case of favouritism. One of the councillors had a nephew who was married on the Saturday and a few days later moved into a three bedroom council house. Yet couples with kids, similar to Jean, were being denied tenancies.

The best they could do was to get a private rented house when it came empty. But Jean couldn't even manage that. Her face, or that of her husband, didn't fit!

I wrote all this down and spent the rest of the evening putting it all together, and writing the letter to the Parish Clerk for it to be read at the next Parish meeting. Parish Council Meetings were held in the local infant's school, and on the evening of the meeting Jean went along to hear her letter read out to all present. Poor thing! She told me that she left the meeting because there was a lot of shouting and she was feeling afraid. Next day, one of the councillors called to see her and wanted to know who had written the letter. He said to her, "I'll bet tha's been to see a lawyer, an't tha?"

"No I haven't," Jean replied.

"Well, who's wrote that letter for thi?" the councillor demanded. "Because thy an't."

"Joe Kenyon did it for me," she said.

"Aw..." the councillor grunted, and then walked away.

Two weeks later she got her council house, and poor little Joe earned the undying, life-long hatred of the councillors. Which I didn't mind one bit.

# THE FACE OF DEATH

During my time as a door trapper, blasting and rock shifting had been going on for six months. The level where I worked was being widened so that double rail tracks and an endless rope could be installed. When that was done, self-operating doors were put in and this meant that my door trapping job was finished.

Although I was yet only 14, I was offered a job as a scraper-lad on a new longwall face that had been opened. The coal face was 120 yards long and manned by 18 colliers. The coal was still hand-got, with pick and shovel, muscle and blood. But the old system of filling coal directly into the tub – a small truck – was done away with and the coal was shovelled onto a conveyor belt running the length of the face. At that time, the belts were installed within six-foot wide steel frames, with side irons and pulleys. The coal was shovelled onto the top belt and some fell onto the bottom belt. The spillage was carried back to the "tension end" – the return drum for the belt – and if it was not prevented from going into the drum-end it would eventually clog it up and either stop the belt or break it. There were times when I had to let the spillage break the belt, so I could have a stop too.

It was the scraper lad's job to keep the tension-end clear of spillage and to prevent the drum from choking up. This was done by fixing at an angle, across the bottom belt near to the drum, what was known as a split bar, normally used to timber the face. This was a piece of timber, four feet six inches wide and two and a half inches thick. Using six-inch nails, I would hammer the bar to a couple of pit props, set tight, one at each side of the belt. At my side, the "gob" side where I worked, the bar was pressed down hard onto the belt so that the spillage was scraped off and stopped from going into the tension end.

The bottom belt was only about three inches from the floor, so it didn't take long before the spillage piled up and overflowed the scraper bar and piled up into the tension-end. Conveyor belts were not always kept in good condition, and it so happened that where a bad length of belt was travelling along the topside there was an excessive amount of spillage onto the bottom belt. The more in haste the colliers shovelled, the more spillage there was, and the more I had to shovel like hell to keep the tension clear. Sometimes, the coal came so fast and thick, it buried my knees, and a collier had to climb over the belt and give me a hand. It was often said that a scraper lad filled more coal than any ten colliers. I reckon it was all that maniac shovelling that developed my arms and shoulders.

At the beginning of the shift I was always first onto the face. My first job was to fix the scraper over the belt: a fresh bar every shift, because they would wear down during the day's scraping. Then I used to fold my jacket and shirt to sit or kneel on, depending upon the amount of spillage coming back. Sometimes there was very little spillage because the colliers would be timbering or using their picks to loosen coal, and so I would sit, legs outstretched and wide apart. Then, holding my shovel under the belt, I would wait until it was full and throw the coal onto the top belt. At other times, the spillage came so thick and fast I had to get onto my knees and shovel like hell. It is much easier to shovel on your knees than standing. Try it!

The day I write about was early in February 1930. As I crawled onto the face – the coal seam was only two foot nine inch thick[4] – I noticed that the air this morning was a bit fresh. One of the odd things you learn about pit atmospheres is the changing pattern of freshness or staleness of the air. Air pressure, weather patterns and other technical reasons too complicated to explain here cause this. Anyway, the air this morning felt fresh, or maybe it was because I was feeling fit and fresh myself. I fixed the scraper, singing as I worked, and waited for the belt to start up. But it never did. Not this morning. Because, just as the colliers were about to come onto the face, a weight started.[5] As the rock overhead cracked and thundered, thick long slivers of razor-sharp, wedge-shaped rock slithered down from the roof.

I had crawled down the face a few yards, mooching about in the gob. ("Gob" is a term pit men use to describe the empty wasteland left behind after the coal has been extracted and the face advanced.) I was about to scurry back towards the tail gate (the roadway leading away from the coalface) when I heard one of the colliers – Terry Mulligan – shout "Joey, bring your bloody self out of there! Can't you hear the face is on the weight". I didn't need telling. That's why I was scurrying as fast as I could crawl towards the tail gate. Then suddenly there was a terrific crack of thunder and as the weight intensified the roof spilt open and daggers of rock sank to the floor.

I crouched down, saw the roof breaking and falling and wondered, fearfully, which bloody way do I go now? The face was weighting on both sides of me. I was in the gob, the most dangerous part of a coal face. Can I make it to the tailgate? No! Then there was another bang as more of the face caved in. That decided me. I turned and scurried back down the face, but it was just the same there. It was only a second or two, but it seemed an age as I crouched there wondering which way to go. There seemed to be no escape. I thought, this is how a little rabbit must feel when it is hemmed in by its hunters. I could feel the face heaving, the thud and the crack of the weight was frightening. Death winked at me. Then, without knowing how I got there, I found myself in a dummy gate. Dummy gates are made when they open up a new coal face by blasting out a section of the roof at a width of eight feet and a height of half a yard. The rock that is blown down, is then used to form a pack: a dry wall of stone, lining each side of the gate. It is put there as a form of weight control to hold up the roof and take some of the pressure off the face. They were called dummy gates because they were allowed to close in as the face advanced. Entries to the dummy gates were spaced along the face, 20 yards apart.

I crawled up the gate for about 30 yards, thinking I would be safe from the weight because I was now in an area where the face had advanced and the roof had gradually settled to the floor. It looked as if the coalface and the gates or tunnels leading to it were closing in, and my only way of escape would be to go up the dummy gate and pray that I could get through. I never bothered to think if there would be a way through; I just knew it was the only way I could go.

For about a hundred yards I was able to crawl with my lamp hung on my neckstrap. But the further I went, the lower the roof became, and the sides were beginning to close in too, so that the height of the gate was not only lower, it was also getting narrower. Now I was unable to crawl any further, so I had to stretch myself out and pull myself along as best I could. It was too low for my lamp to be hung round my neck and I had to hold it by its base and push it forward as I crouched even lower. It was only because of my small size that I had been able to get up the gate as far as this. A bigger chap could not have made it. Unable to crawl, I was stretched out, lying on my belly, edging myself forward inch by inch. Then it got to the stage where I had to tilt my lamp because of the jutting stones protruding from the roof which was little more than a foot high. A couple of times I burned my hands as I tried to hold the lamp by the middle. My hand ached because of the strain of holding the lamp by the base and trying to balance it. Once, the lamp slipped and fell over. I grabbed it in panic and blew frantically through the lamp vents to get the flame stable again.

I suddenly realised that it was impossible for me to turn around and go back. There was only one way and that was forward, whatever lay in front of me. I sobbed a little, my body utterly exhausted, and didn't want to move ever again. But I knew that I had to keep going. And I could only do this by carefully moving my lamp forward, making sure it didn't fall over; then, by gripping the floor and pushing with my feet, I pushed and dragged myself along, belly scraping the floor and my back catching the rough edges of the roof. The distance seemed to be miles and miles and miles, and never ending. Every inch I managed to pull myself forward called for my utmost effort.

I discovered later that my chest, belly and knees were cut and badly grazed where the rough ground had peeled off the skin. My back was full of cuts where the sharp protruding knife-edges of stone had cut into my flesh or scraped off the skin. By now my body was aching, sweat was pouring from me, every inch was a mile. But yet I never had a thought that I would not get through.

Suddenly I thought I saw a flash of light. I must be near the cross-gate, I thought. I shouted, and shouted again. I listened. But there was nothing. I had the feeling that the air had freshened a bit. I knew that I could only be a matter of feet away from the opening at the end of the dummy gate. I pushed myself forward a few more inches. Then I stopped. It was not only the pain; I was feeling desperately tired and just wanted to go to sleep. For a while I lay still, my arm curled around my head. It was an effort to lift my face and look ahead.

There was nothing to look at. Just a blackness that said nothing. I put my face back to the floor, sobbing a little, and listened to my breathing. I watched the puff of dust around my face as my breathing disturbed it. I could hear my heart pounding in my ears. Then I thought of home, my Mum and Dad and the kids. Then, startled, I knew I heard something. I squinted forward. Was I dreaming? Yes, I saw a flicker of light, and then it went. I could hear footsteps, running. I shouted and shouted; my lungs fit to burst. The light came again, got brighter, then it passed. I knew now that I was at the end of the gate, just a matter of feet away, because I had seen the light and could feel the freshness of the air. I knew that there was an opening into the crossgate. Energy poured into me. I pushed and pulled myself with renewed strength. Cooler air caressed my face. I sobbed, I cried.

Then I heard another voice and a brighter dancing light loomed before me. Again I shouted "'ello, 'ello, 'ello!" The light went; then came back.

I heard a voice say, "Did you hear summat?" Then a lamp held close to the floor appeared. I saw a face peering through the hole.

"It's me, Joey Kenyon!" I shouted.

"Is that Joey?" It was Jack Booth who shouted back to me.

"How the bloody hell has tha got up there?" Then Jack shouted to someone "Go round and tell the Deputy we've found him, he's come up the bloody dummy gate".

I edged myself forward to the opening, "Grinning all over my clock," as Jack Booth put it. He reached out, got hold of my hands and pulled me through into the crossgate.

The time was just after ten o'clock. It had taken me four hours to crawl and scrape 200 yards up the dummy gate. I stood up in the gate and stretched a little, just for the sheer joy of it.

"Do you feel alright lad?" Jack Booth asked. Then another chap arrived and gave me a bottle of water. I just simply poured it down my throat. Ooh! I couldn't stop drinking. Never, ever, was there a sweeter elixir than that long drink of cool water.

Then, with a mixture of admonishings, jokes and laughter, the Deputy dabbed my cuts and grazes with iodine.

"Where's your clothes Joey? I couldn't find them in the gate," Jack asked.

"I left them on the face."

"Well, you won't see them again lad", the Deputy said. "The top half of the face has completely come in. We've being trying to find a way through. We thought you were a gonner."

When the Deputy had cleaned me up a bit more he told a couple of men to take me to the pit bottom. "Your Dad is waiting for you on the pit top," he said.

When I got to the pit bottom I was told it was cold and had been snowing all morning. I was stripped to the waist; my shirt, jacket and other clothes were buried forever on the face. One of the lads in the pit bottom, Bill Ride, lent me his pullover, a jacket and a cap, to go home in.

What a joy it was, when I stepped off the chair, and walked through the doors into the wonderful daylight. The air was sweet and fresh, snow was falling gently, and it seemed to be saying, "Welcome!" Never was a time so beautiful as it was on that blissful morning. The sweetest moment of my life.

Dad was there, tears in his eyes. He put his arms around me, and we walked home.

I reckon that only such a naive little scrap as I was would have attempted – dared – to go up a dummygate 200 yards advanced from the coal face.

Normally they close down as the roof settles and meets the floor.

Many's the time I have wondered about the risk I had taken – was forced to take really. I had nightmares about it for years after. I could have knocked my lamp out. Stale air or gas could have put it, or me, out. There might not have been a way through to the crossgate. There was certainly no way I could have gone back, even if I had the strength left to do it. I would be lying there yet, squeezed out of existence. But, at the time, it never occurred to me that I would not get through.

# MY FIRST HOLIDAY

My first long trip on my bike was when Ernie Spooner asked me to take his step-son, Joe Lowe, to visit his oldest daughter at Cullercoates, near Whitley Bay. It was Barnsley Feast week, mid-August 1931. The Barnsley pits closed down for the Feast Week, but there was no holiday with pay in those days. All so-called holidays, like Bank Holidays, were just another period when you were out of work. So there was no real holiday: you couldn't afford one.

Joe and I became firm friends because we worked together in the pit. He lived at Grimethorpe, where his step-dad was a coal cutter, driving one of the early, noisy, dusty machines that were being introduced into the pits, where long-wall coal faces were being developed. Ernie Spooner, as I have mentioned earlier, became my mentor, educator and guide to my reading. He died of pneumoconiosis later. He was a Geordie. He had previously worked at a pit in Durham, but had been blacked by management and denied work at the pit. Like many others, driven out for their militancy, he came to work in the pits around Barnsley and Doncaster. Anyway, Ernie bought Joe a bike to go to work on and, because it was nearing Barnsley Feast Week, he asked if I would take Joe to Cullercoates for a free holiday to stay with his oldest daughter who lived there.

Unluckily for Joe though, his bike was a heavy "sit-up-and-beg", as we used to call them – OK for going to work on but not much good for long distance riding – whereas my bike was a sleek, light, racing model with a fixed gear. We set off this Saturday morning at 8am to bike up the A1 to Newcastle. Well, not quite to Newcastle, because we had promised to see an uncle who lived in a village called Hunwick, in Durham County. He kept a pub named the Wheatsheaf Arms and Joe and I would spend a night there.

Poor young Joe was not used to long journeys. His bike was heavy, he got tired and it rained for most of the journey. Twice he fell asleep and fell off. It was hard for me as well, because I had to keep treading the pedals and waiting for him. We had done most of the journey, and then I spotted a small road-side café. It was a better class café than the usual run-of-the-mill transport beans-on-toast joint. The café was empty and, as we walked in, a pretty young girl, dressed in a neat black dress and a white laced trimmed pinafore came to serve us. She must have felt sorry for the two pathetic, drenched young lads because, after she had taken our order, she came back with the proprietor of the café: a very attractive, middle aged woman.

"Oh, my dears," she exclaimed, "you look wet through, and I'll bet you are cold as well. Come and sit by the fire."

She then brought us a good meal of lamb chops and veg, followed by a huge, delicious sweet. I looked at Joe, and said in a whisper, "I dunt know how much this is going to cost." But there was no need for us to worry. The kind lady wouldn't take a penny from us. Indeed she made us a sandwich to take away with us.

We said our goodbyes and resumed our journey on the last lap to Hunwick. Joe seemed to be in better shape after the short doze he had by the fire. Finally we arrived at the Wheatsheaf. Joe's Aunt, Mrs Grayson, welcomed us profusely, fussing round, taking our damp clothes to dry and fixing us up with something warm to wear. Mr Grayson – John, a friendly, serious man – wanted to help warm us up with a large whisky, "to keep a cold away" as he put it. But whisky was not to our taste, not yet anyway. So Mrs Grayson gave us some ginger wine instead, and that was powerful stuff indeed. Then we had a lovely supper of thick slices of home cured ham, pickled onions and other trimmings. And then, having wrapped ourselves around that, we washed it down with a drop of good ale. We spent the evening in the tap room, playing darts and chatting with the locals. There's nowt like being in good friendly company.

Next morning, bright and early, we had a good, filling breakfast, and prepared to resume our journey. The bikes had had a good soaking, so we decided to give them a polish, and to oil the axles and the chain etc. John didn't have any oil, but Mrs Grayson brought us some caster oil and asked if that would do. "Yes" I said, "It'll do fine." It certainly made the bikes run more smoothly.

Our next stop was to be at Gateshead, where we were to call in and say hello to some other relations. We stayed at Gateshead for an hour and Joe's uncle there offered to escort us to Cullercoats. We stopped on the bridge at Newcastle, to admire and wonder at its structure, although I did think it looked a bit clumsy and not really very aesthetic. The view was interesting though – the many houses rising from the banks, the ships on the water – a fresh and captivating experience. Then we pushed on to another unforgettable memory: the ride down that long, straight, concrete road, leading to Tynemouth. At first I thought I could see a massive field, dotted with dark humps of some sort, and then, as I got nearer, I recognised that it was the sea. My very first sight of the sea! Can't say how excited I felt at that moment. The smell of it, the sound of the seagulls, the tang of fresh air, were a whole new experience.

At Tynemouth we turned left and rode up the coast road to Cullercoats. Our arrival at the home of Joe's sister, Alice, again gave us a marvellous welcome, and at once I felt relaxed and comfortable. Alice was a tall, graceful woman, about 30, who spoke in a soft, gentle manner. I liked her at once. Her husband was a friendly, boisterous sort of chap who had been a fisherman, but now worked in the office at the local railway station. We got on very well. He showed us around Cullercoats and took us down to the small quayside to look at the small boats moored there. He had two brothers, both fishermen, and they arranged to take us out one night to do a spot of fishing. Joe and I weren't much use though. He spent most of his time heaving over the side of the boat. I tried to be helpful but, not knowing the ropes, there wasn't much I could do. But the experience was good. Looking towards the shore at the lights, especially the flash of the lighthouse, gave me a new kind of perspective offering new possibilities, especially when I thought of the work in the pit.

We came ashore early in the morning and went to the market, fascinated at the sight of the fishermen laying out their catch of many kinds of fish, mostly cod, but also crabs and lobsters. The men bargained for whatever price they could get. Joe and I then went back to Alice's, all damp and stinking of fish. Alice had a good laugh at us, filled us up with breakfast and then packed us off to bed for a couple of hours.

Within the small bay there was a handy jetty which I used quite a lot. When the tide was in, it was a perfect diving and swimming place. The water was crystal clear and when I dived deep into it, spectators had a clear view of me performing my twists and turns and other swimming tricks as I came up to the surface. I was quite a show-off, known at home for my swimming and diving skills.

We stayed on at Cullercoats until Wednesday and then we hiked to Chopwell, a mining village somewhere to the west of Newcastle. Joe had some relations there and it had been arranged for us to visit them. We had arranged to stay for a couple of days, but they all wanted us to stay longer. Again, we were made a great fuss of and everybody was friendly. Especially the young lads of the locality. They used to stand around admiring my bike. It all seemed something new to them. None of them seemed to have bikes. A lot of the men were out of work and no doubt bikes were something they couldn't afford. In spite of all this, we were more than welcome and could share whatever they had. The lads were fascinated by the white flash fixed on the back mudguard of my bike. It was a piece of celluloid stuff, about a foot long and three inches wide, and had a red heart at the base of the flash. I told the lads that the flash meant I was a member of the red heart gang. They were duly impressed and envious of my apparent good fortune.

The family that was putting us up had a daughter, Mary, aged 16. We struck up an immediate friendship and, on the Wednesday evening, she let me take her to the pictures. It was the first date I had ever had with a girl and I liked it. The next day Joe and I visited other relations around the village and Mary escorted us all the way. In the evening she readily accepted my invitation to take her for a walk across the fields. We walked hand in hand, through a couple of fields, and then into the woods, drawing ever closer together. Then I put my arms around her shoulders, with the back of my hand under her chin. I then slowly and gently pressed her chin upwards, and as she leaned back, I softly lowered her onto the ground. We lay together facing each other and I gently caressed her face, saying nice things to her. Then we talked and laughed, and gently wrestled each other, and I experienced my first-ever kiss. Time moved swiftly on, and we realised that we had to get back home. We strolled arm in arm. How short a mile can be, when your walk is such a pleasure.

When we got home, Mary's mum seemed quite anxious because we had stayed out so long. I said I was sorry, but we had forgotten the time and had walked further than we intended to. She had no cause for concern though. We were just a couple of naïve sixteens, not fully wised up about love and sex, even though the emotions were there. We were more restrained and disciplined than the kids of today. They have it pumped into them every day from the tabloids, magazines and telly-films. There have been many gains for people in modern times, but there have been losses too.

Mary and I had a wonderful time together, short as it was. And I promised her faithfully that I would write to her and come up to Chopwell again to see her. And I never did.

# BOBBIES, BAD AND GOOD

Sometimes on a Sunday I would go for a long ride on my bike, dressed only in slippers, brown shorts and a summer vest. It was very daring those days, not to be fully dressed, even though you were on your bike. This was a hot summer day and I decided to ride to Harrogate. Setting off just after breakfast, I had an hour or so in Harrogate, and then after a bite and a cuppa set off home again. Working in the pit, the sun rarely gets to your skin, so on my way back, to get a bit more of it, I took my vest off and stuffed it in my saddle-bag. I was riding through Wakefield, near to the Cathedral, when a bobby signalled me to stop. He asked me where I was going, and where I had been, and then he accused me of being indecently dressed.

"How do you mean?" I asked.

The bobby, sweating cobs in his heavy uniform, nearly exploded, and said, "You have only a pair of slippers on and a pair of shorts! You are improperly dressed. You'd better get home and get some clothes on. If I see you like that again I'll run you in."

On another occasion – I was 17 at the time – I had been on a long Sunday ride through Penistone, Tintwistle, Mossley, Holmfirth and home to Barnsley. I was riding on my last bit of the journey, along Wakefield Road, just before the turn-off down to our village, and a car passed me. Fifty yards on, the car stopped and a bobby got out and signalled me to stop. He had a local farm owner with him, who was driving the car. The bobby, a big, fat, red-nosed copper, asked me what I was playing at.

"I'm not playing at owt," I said. "I'm just going home."

"You were riding recklessly. You could have caused an accident." There wasn't anything or anybody in sight. Roads were quiet in those days; quiet enough to play whip and top, as we used to do. Then the farmer said, "You were riding recklessly."

"I wasn't," I replied.

The bobby then asked for my name and address, and said he would be reporting me.

Two or three weeks later I got a summons on blue paper, telling me to attend the Magistrates' Court on a charge of pedalling a bicycle furiously.

'Strewth – pedalling a bicycle furiously at the end of a 70 mile run?

Along I went to the court, losing a day's work and wages, and was arraigned before a grim-looking fearsome threesome of magistrates. The bobby, licking his finger, began to recite how he was proceeding in a car driven by Mr Farmer along Wakefield Road, near Staincross junction, and witnessed the said Joseph Kenyon riding a bicycle furiously along Wakefield Road and likely to cause an accident.

The Chairman of the bench looked at me, gave me a lecture, and then said, "Have you any questions to ask the constable?"

I was flabbergasted. "He's telling lies…" And that's as far as I got, because the Chairman interrupted me saying, "I don't want a statement. Have you got any 'questions' to ask the constable?" Well I didn't know how to ask a question, and every time I tried to say something, I was told smartly to shut up.

I was duly found guilty of pedalling a bicycle furiously, and fined ten shilling and £4 costs to cover the loss of the farmer's earnings for that morning. £4/10s! How the hell did they think I could pay that? It was about 10 weeks' pocket money and about three weeks' wages. I couldn't pay it, and I wasn't going to. Several times through the following year a bobby called to collect the fine, but I wouldn't pay it. Then, one Monday morning, I bumped into the Bailiff and he carted me off to Armley Jail in Leeds, where I spent a relaxing 7 days sewing mailbags. I could go on about the food as well, but don't want to turn your stomach.

Mind you, there are good bobbies as well as bad ones. While I was living in Slough I went to work one morning at 8 a.m. and learned that the factory was closed for the day. Summat wrong with the power supply. So I nipped back to my digs, changed into my riding gear – slippers, khaki shorts and a sleeveless white summer shirt – and set off for a ride to Bognor Regis. Had a nice day there: a bit of swimming, dozing on the beach, strolling round the shops. And then, after tea, I set off back to Slough. I was well on my way towards Guildford and approaching a small township when it grew dark, so I switched on my bike lamp. But there was no light: just a faint glimmer. The battery had conked out. I kept on riding steadily, hoping I might see a place where I could get a new battery. But no luck. Then a copper spotted me. I stopped and asked him where I could buy a new battery. He looked at my lamp, and said, ever so friendly like, "You won't get one now young man. The shops are closed." Then he paused and said "Come along with me".

"I hope he's not going to bloody lock me up," I thought. But he took me to his home. A nice, comfortable, homely home it was too; with a pleasant, comfy, buxom, house-proud wife, ever so pleasant and not a bit like a southerner. She made me a nice supper and packed me a sandwich as well. While this was happening the policeman, lovely bloke, had oiled my bike, and put a new battery in my lamp. Later he showed me to the main road and set me off to Guildford. So, you see, there are good'uns, as well as bad'uns.

# TRAMMING

Tramming was just about the most painful and soul destroying job in a pit. Only pits such as the two we had in our village employed trammers. Other better maintained pits nearby had high and wide roadways and used pit ponies to pull the coal tubs from the coal face to the haulage where, by a system of winches or endless ropes, they were pulled into the pit bottom and then whisked up the pit shaft and out of the pit. But our pits used muscle and blood. Our blood. A trammer had to be fit, broad backed and short. He was usually in his late teens or early twenties. Strong in muscle and bone, and a bit weak in the head.

At the age of fifteen I joined a Health and Strength Club. The subs were sixpence a week and it was run by its members in an old chapel hall. I spent two hours a day there during the week, and three hours each Saturday and Sunday – mainly skipping, wrestling and weight lifting. I also punched the ball a bit. That way I developed a strong back and strong muscles in my arms and legs. For me, being only five feet four, very fit and strong, tramming was a doddle. Getting a tub up and down the gate quickly enabled me to help my mate with coal getting and earn a couple of bob extra

A trammer's job was to push or 'tram' an empty coal tub up the gate and into the bank. The bank was a short coalface, about ten yards wide, worked by two men, the filler and the trammer. The older less agile man worked at the face all shift, getting the coal and filling the tubs; the young mate fetched the tubs into the bank, helped with the filling and then whizzed down the gate, taking the full tub into a main road, known as the level, from which it was hauled by winch into the pit bottom in loads of twenty tubs at a time.

The gate, as it was known, was a kind of tunnel leading up to the bank, or face. It was just high enough and wide enough to allow a tub to scrape through. If a tub got fast – stuck between the roof and the floor – there was no way you could get past it. If you wanted to get out, you had to crawl back up the gate – two hundred yards or more – into the bank, then crawl through the gob which was the waste land left after the coal had been got out, and then into the next bank and down their gate.

A coal tub is a miniature wagon made to hold an estimated eight hundredweight of coal. Some tubs were made of metal and others of wood. It was the wooden ones which mostly got stuck, because some were an inch higher than the metal ones. They were much heavier to push as well. Tubs measured two feet six inches wide, two feet six inches high and about three feet six inches long, and they only just scraped through. The slightest movement of the roof, sides or floor and they got fast. Because the gates were so inadequate, ventilation was very poor; it was hot and steamy work. The coal face was a yard and three inches high which didn't leave much room for the filler to throw his coal into the tub. You could make a bit more space by lifting the tub off the rail track at one end and placing its wheels on the floor.

If everything went okay, the conditions were good and there were no hold-ups because of tubs getting fast, we could get about four tons of coal each shift. Four hard-gotten, back-breaking tons. We were paid two shillings and two pence per ton, with sometimes a stoppage taken out of that if the weigh-man thought the tub was a bit on the heavy side and that a bit of stone had been added.

For tramming we were paid a sliding rate, depending upon the distance. For the first 40 yards we got nothing, after another 25 yards we got three halfpence, and then for every extra 25 yards a penny. So for tramming a tub up and back down the gate, around 400 yards, we could earn an extra seven pence a tub. This was regarded as poor compensation for extra tramming, because while we were tramming we were not getting coal and wages would suffer. There were other jobs too: trimming, timbering, fetching materials and moving the face railtrack nearer to the face as we advanced. These helped to make up the wages a bit, but they were hard-fought gains which the boss begrudged, and there was nothing extra for towing your guts out on a tub that was fast. At the end of a good day, we could maybe earn up to twelve shillings a shift. But good days were few and far between. Sometimes, when the going was rough and dangerous, although we worked a damn sight harder, lost gallons of sweat and sometimes blood, working for nowt, we had to fall back on the 'mini' or minimum wage of eight shillings a shift.

The trammer usually suffered most, towing his rope out, shredding his back against the roof when a lousy tub got fast and wouldn't move: nowt paid for this. When a tub stuck between the floor and the roof it was reported to the deputy, a pit official in charge of that district within the pit. He reported it to the manager, who gave orders to the nightshift deputy to send a dinter in. A dinter was usually an elderly man, on a low day wage, who worked regular nights. He was usually past doing heavy work but useful for doing odd repair jobs that had been reported from the dayshift. One of these was to go into the bank gate where a tub was fast and lower the rail track an inch or two to allow the tub to go free. Pit owners were very begrudging about paying for this work. They would have the repair man skimp jobs and make-do.

The ground in a pit was always on the move. The floor would lift, sometimes because of rising gas, sometimes because of the roof pressing the sides and forcing the floor upwards. The dinter would crawl up the gate where a mark had been left or where he could see there was a tub still fast. Using his pick, he would dig and scrape out the floor under the sleepers so as to lower the track an inch or two. A makeshift job, but the absolute maximum allowed by the boss. To do a good and lasting job would take time and cost more money than the deputy was allowed to pay for it. It was easier and cheaper to let the trammer pay in sweat, blood and sometimes tears.

Coal seams are usually on an incline, a slight gradient of about 1 in 20. Banks were organised to commence from the upside of a level. It was easier to push an empty tub than a full tub up the incline. It was also easier to slide along the plates holding onto a full tub and let it go down the gate pulled by its own weight. (The "plates" are the rails which came in lengths of six feet or nine feet and were nailed to wooden sleepers.) Because the gates were so low – only two feet six inches – the best way to travel up or down the gate, was to push a tub, or ride the plates holding onto a tub. The alternative was to crawl on your knees and this can be very uncomfortable, especially over rough ground.

As a trammer, I had to wear clogs to be able to 'slide the plates'. Besides the iron on the outer edge of the clog there was also an inner iron. Inside the inner iron, I would nail a piece of tin which I had cut to size. Whenever I was taking a tub down the gate I would grab hold of the handles – there were two at each end – give it a push to start it down the incline of the track, then quickly jump on to the plates, with one foot at an angle so I could push my tin piece against the plate and gain some control over the speed of the tub as it hurtled down the gate. I kept my head well down below the level of the tub. A slight raising of the head in a moment of forgetfulness could result in a swift scalping. The easiest way to push a tub up the gate was to lean low into the back of it and push with your head, resting your hands on the buffers. To protect my head and hair I wore a 'bannicker' – a small skull cap cut from an old trilby and fashioned to fit on the head without slipping off.

Some trammers just wore their day caps, but a bannicker was more comfortable and less sweaty.

The end of a shift was always welcome, especially when your muscles and bones ached like hell. When I got home I had my dinner and then, before I started to drop off with sheer exhaustion, I would go into the kitchen (a bath or a shower would have been heaven), strip off to my waist and wash my head, arms and chest over the stone kitchen sink. There, while I leaned over the sink, my dear Ma would ever so tenderly wash my back, using a flannel or a piece of lint, wiping around or gently swabbing the cuts and scabs down my spine.

Sometimes, when I went to the pictures, I would forget myself and carelessly drop down onto the seat. I would curse and grunt as I felt the sudden pain of the sores on my back. There were times when, without thinking, I'd shuffle my back against a chair, especially if it was itching. Then blood would trickle out as I opened up the sores, and I'd have to change my vest and shirt and have my back cleaned. If I didn't do that right away, my clothes would stick to my back and it would be much harder – painful too – getting them off without starting the bleeding again. When they did get stuck the best way of getting my vest and shirt off was to dab over the cuts with a piece of lint soaked in warm water until they were softened, and then very slowly peel off the vest and shirt so as not to re-open the wounds. That was always painful. Even lying in bed you had to be careful about opening up wounds and feeling the pain of them when trying to turn over.

One day my mate had a "laker" – a day off work. It was Wednesday, and quite common for colliers to have a laker on a Wednesday, especially if they had been having a rough time of it for a shift or two. Normally a man wasn't allowed to work in a bank on his own, but the deputy allowed me to go in. I'd filled a couple of tubs, taken them down the gate and fetched up a couple of empties. I filled my third tub, went down the gate with it, speeding along for about a hundred yards, when scrunch! – the tub got fast. I shoved my back against it with my feet spragged against a sleeper, but it wouldn't shift. I tried pulling it back, shaking and cursing it, but it was stuck fast and staying stuck.

There was nothing I could do but crawl back up the gate into the face and fill another tub – I had a couple of spare ones there – and then whip down the gate, letting the tub belt along at its own speed, desperately holding on to the handles, all tensed up for the inevitable crunch as it hit the immovable tub. BANG! It stopped dead. I could feel my bones flying about the gate, bells rang, lights flashed. I flopped down for some ten minutes, lying on the floor and cursing myself, the tub and the lousy pit from here to hell. Eventually I got up, and dragged at the second tub. Thankfully it hadn't got stuck too. I dragged it back for two or three yards and rammed it against the fast tub with all the strength I could muster. The fast tub wouldn'y budge. Again I pulled back the second tub and rammed it again and again. By now I was cursing, sobbing and bleeding; my back cut to ribbons by jagged rocks projecting from the roof and walls.

I crawled my way back up to the face. I had it in my mind what I was going to do. I got into the face, took hold of my hammer and wildly, madly set about skittling the face timber out, pulled down a few rocks and stones from the roof, and filled a third tub with it. Then, raging and fuming, I pushed and tugged at the tub, got it onto the gate track, gave it a massive push and shouted "Gerron! Knock the fucking hole in!"

Having got that off my chest, I had a good swig of water, got dressed, took hold of my pick and shovel, and made my way through the gob and into the next bank.

"Hey up Jooer! What tha doing coming through there?"

"Going home" I said. "Can I put mi tackle on your tub?"

"Tha can tek this tub darn if tha likes, we've got a spare".

I put my pick and shovel on the tub, making sure it was well below the level of the rib sides, and off I went. I made my way to the pit bottom, and the onsetter, the bloke in charge of sending the chair up the shaft, said "Where's tha going?"

"Home," I said.

"'As tha got a note from't Deputy?"

"No I ent seen him."

"Well I can't let thi up then."

"Tha'd better," I said, "I'm badly. If tha dunt let mi art, tha'll be in bother."

I got out of the pit, walked across the pit yard, and, without knocking, entered the manager's office and slung the pick and shovel onto the manager's desk, saying, "Go and get thi own fucking coal."

The manager, known as Cookie by the lads, jumped up and yelled, "What the hell's up wi thi, Jooer?"

"There's a couple o' tubs fast in 428" – the number of the bank where I worked. "There's a couple of tubs fast, and they can fucking stop there for all I care. Tha'll not get me in that gate again for all the tea in China. I'm leaving and I want mi cards."

On the Wednesday, the day I packed it in, I told my Mum that I was

finishing at the pit. "I won't go back there at any price," I said.
Meantime, I was stripping to the waist and as I pulled off my shirt she gasped "Good God lad, what have you done to your back? Come here, let me clean it for you".

"I got a tub fast in the gate and I've done this trying to get it loose. I'm leaving and I'm fetching my cards on Friday." Then I added: "I've been talking to Mr Roach. Their Brian has gone down south to Slough, near London, and he's doing well. Mr Roach told me there's a great new industrial estate being built and there are plenty of jobs."

"When are you going then?" Ma asked.

"Sunday morning," I replied.

# SLOUGH

After breakfast on Sunday morning I stuffed a few things in the saddlebag on my bike, said goodbye to my family and off I went. I arrived in Slough, some two hundred miles away, near about 11 o'clock that night.

I looked in wonder at the dozens of multi-coloured lights surrounding the factories. I could see them before I got into the town. Horlicks was the first one I spotted. Eventually I ended up in Farnham Road and recognised a few illuminated trade names: Aspro, Echo Margarine — what a stink as you passed that place. Then Fine Tubes and 4711, the perfume factory — what a lovely smell!

I finished up in a cafe, crowded with lads and lasses, some in their early twenties, some a bit older. They were mostly on night shift waiting to start work at midnight at Western's biscuit factory. One of them, a lad from Bolton, offered to take me up to his digs. They had room for another lodger and would take me in, he said. I liked the house very much. It was one of the new semi-detached private houses being built at the time to accommodate the influx of workers from Scotland, Wales and the North of England.

Despite much house building, private and Council, almost every house in the town had its lodgers. The digs were 7/6 a week and for that I got free bread, tea or coffee and a Sunday dinner. I bought my own food and Mrs Clatworthy cooked it for me. I had breakfast, tea and supper at the digs and bought my dinner in a large canteen near the factory.

The landlady, a very pleasant good-looking woman in her early thirties, told me that D M Davies, furniture makers, were 'setting on'. I went along, saw one of the foremen, and asked for a job. He wanted to know if I had any tools. "No," I said "I've only just come down from Barnsley, but I'll pay for some if I can draw some from the stores." Mrs Clatworthy had tipped me off about that.

"OK, I'll set you on and you can start now," the foreman said. "I'll give you a note for some tools and you can pay for them out of your wages."

I got a light hammer, two wood chisels, a tenon saw and a veneering knife. I was then shown to a bench where a young chap from Maidenhead was working. We both had to trim and fix the base of Ultra wireless cases to the frame. We each had to do 200 cases a day, 100 in the morning and 100 in the afternoon. After I had been on the job for a couple of weeks, I made some alterations to the jig in which we placed the bases for fixing to the frame. After this adjustment I found that I could easily do 400 cases a day without any effort. Without thinking about the consequences, I just went on happily banging out 400 a day. Too many cases travelling along the line soon choked up the system. Then three men in white coats walked past me a couple of times, watching me working. "They've come to take me away," I thought. Then one of the whitecoats, DMD himself, asked how I managed to get so many cases done at such a pace. I showed them how I had changed the jig and, in effect, doubled production. One of them remarked to the others that the modification meant they'd only need one chap at this bench in future. "Oh dear", I thought. "Now I am creating unemployment; I'll never be forgiven".

DMD said "Show this lad round the factory, try him out on one or two veneering jobs."

I spent two weeks learning about different repair jobs and then was put to work in the repair shop. My job was to repair damaged polished cases: faults caused by poor veneering, blisters in the varnish and a variety of other problems.

Working at DMD's was a pleasure. All the scabs and sores on my back had gone. I could work at my own pace and took a pride in what I was doing. I could work extra hours in the evening and on Sunday morning. I also got a pay rise from 9d an hour to 11d.

It was very handy being able to work late in the evenings because I could do odd repair jobs as favours for the girls in the polishing shop. Some of them would come to me in distress, near to tears, and needed comforting because they had botched up too many jobs that day and didn't want the foreman to know. I received generous compensation from some of them.

I reckon I could have settled in Slough, so far as the work was concerned, but I didn't care for the town or the Sloughites and I never really felt at home. In mid August the factory closed for a week's holiday. I packed a few things, got on my bike and went home to see the family, taking presents for my parents and the kids. I was anxious to see my Dad as well. He was now back home for good.

If you left home and got a job in the South you were regarded as doing well. That's how friends and neighbours thought of me. It was a myth.

Life in the likes of Slough was cold. There was no warmth in the people, no caring, no comradeship. If you said "good morning" to anyone, they looked at you with suspicion as though you were after something or a bit touched. Mention the words 'trade union' at work and people backed off as though you had the plague.

Anyway, I was at home, on holiday and away from all that. One evening in the club I was just about to order a pint and who should come up to me, but old Cookie, the pit manager. "Let me get that Joe," he said. And then those boring words: "I hear you are doing very well for yourself these days".

"Well, it's not so bad. I like the work; it calls for some skill and I find it very relaxing after tramming. But I would still prefer to be in Barnsley."

"Have you thought about coming back to the pit then, Joe?"

"I've thought about it. In fact sometimes I miss it. But I don't suppose tha'll find me a job again?"

"Oh I don't know. You are a good strong lad. I've always admired you in spite of your cussedness. We could do with some good fillers. There's no tramming now; it's all longwall faces. Tha coal is under-cut and blasted. All they have to do is just sling it on to the belt."

"Well in that case, I'll come back. But I'll have to nip back to Slough first. I'll need my cards and I've a few things to fetch as well."

On the Monday I went back to Slough, went into DMD's and gave them two hours notice that I was leaving. The foreman tried to talk me out of leaving. Then he fetched the manager who offered me a two pence an hour rise in wages, and then a second two pence an hour. But I said, "Thank you, I am sorry, but I'm needed back home."

# BACK TO THE PIT

Pit work is a dirty dangerous job, but it is also a challenge, no matter how much you hate it and want to leave it. If you did get away you yearned to get back to it. Killings and accidents were common, part of the life you learned to live with. Every working day, two or more miners were killed while doing their work somewhere within the industry, and many thousands more were maimed and crippled. And that's not counting those who went down with pneumaconiosis and other killer lung diseases. Very few families were not touched by death or serious accident at some time or other. Every village had its quota of men and young lads with broken backs, a leg or an arm missing, hands crushed and useless – many of them still fighting for compensation with the compensation doctor who also was an employee of the company.

When a chap was killed, not only his family, but his mates and indeed the whole village grieved for him and for his widow and children. Out of respect and sympathy for them, work was stopped for 24 hours, and an agreed deduction of a shilling per man and sixpence per boy was taken from the wages to be paid to the widow or next of kin. Collections were also taken round the village.

If the accident or death was caused by the negligence of the employer the odds of winning compensation were stacked against you. The company used every ruse and dodge, even lying or bribing witnesses to lie; anything to stop the widow from getting compensation.

When I went back to the pit, to work as a filler on a longwall face it was a damn site easier and less painful than tramming. The coal face, 120 yards long, had already been undercut by a coal-cutting machine which travelled along it, cutting a band of stone and coal out at the base of the seam, about five inches thick to a depth of five feet. The coal cutter was a clumsy chunk of steel about nine feet long, two feet wide and two feet high. It was an ugly, noisy, grinding hell of a machine and choked the cutting team with dust.

Before the coal was cut, a borer would traverse the face, drilling holes four feet six inches in depth and nine feet apart. After the coal was undercut, and the conveyor belt moved up to the face, a shot firer would stem the holes with explosives[6] and blast the coal. If he was good at his job, the shot firer would blast the coal just sufficiently to break it up and make it easier for the filler to shovel it onto the moving belt.

Filling coal that had been undercut and blasted was a lot easier and less painful than tramming, but it was still bloody hard graft. The height at the face was only three feet, and when you had slung 17 tons of coal at a mad pace, on your knees all shift, you weren't as fresh as a daisy. Indeed there were times when it really got dog rough: the roof might be fractured and be unsafe. The coal cutter may not have done his job well; the borer may have drilled the holes at the wrong angle and the wrong depth, or too far apart; or the shot firer may not have stemmed the shots well enough. Any of these mishaps could make the shift for the filler one long cursing misery.

I was twenty-one and had been filling for a year, when the pit suffered an almighty explosion. It happened at 3 a.m. on the morning of August 6, 1936: 58 men were killed outright — all within a matter of seconds. Many of them were smashed and battered almost beyond recognition. The explosion (some accounts say there were two) was so fierce and dreadful that its effects could be seen nearly two miles from the spot at which it took place — nearly two miles along an underground roadway a thousand feet down.

There was one survivor, an engine driver, and he was found bruised and battered, lying 1800 yards from the centre of the blast. He died later in hospital. The mutilated bodies lay in groups of three or four. Some lay singly within a few yards of each other. When SOS messages were sent out to neighbouring pits hundreds of miners rushed to help. They stood in line at the pithead, waiting to be called. Silent crowds of men, women and children stood around. Agonised faces, women stifling their tears, children crying, waiting to see if their loved ones might be brought out alive.

Four men had amazing luck. Half an hour before the explosion, they unexpectedly finished their work and left the pit. One of them returned as a member of the rescue team.

"It is impossible for anyone to escape," they said. Yet, in the days that followed the crowds waited, and the rain fell ceaselessly. On their way back from the pithead the rescue workers walked grimly past the waiting crowd. Many were longing to call out for news, but no one did. One of the unbearable agonies about a pit disaster is the intensity and the silence of the waiting — more in dread than in patience: lest the question asked should bring an answer that snuffs out that last flicker of hope.

Doctor Jimmy Henderson, the local village doctor, was among the rescue workers. On emerging from the pit five hours later, he said that it was hopeless. Most of the dead he had seen had been torn to pieces by the force of the blast: others were lying about in attitudes of suffocation brought about by carbon-monoxide poisoning. "All along the roadways," he reported, "There were piles of rubble where the roof had collapsed. Coal tubs had been hurled about and smashed. All this, and the gas-filled air, made it impossible to get to the men."

From the first day, ambulances stood by, but no bodies came up. The crowds of relatives, neighbours and many others waiting in sympathy, grew so large that the area had to be roped off to allow free passage for the rescue workers through the black mud to the pithead. And behind that rope, the crowd stood, under the ceaseless rain, hour by hour, day by day, until the waiting turned to grieving – no crying – as the rescuers began to bring the bodies up. The local school nearby was taken over and prepared to receive them. More than forty nurses from miles around the area came in to help the doctors.

Yet all this death, all this pain and suffering, because it was so vast, was not regarded by the law as accidental but as an 'act of God'. And therefore compensation was not payable.

A year after the explosion, my Dad was killed on the pit top. He was looking for pieces of coal to give us a fire. The door of a wagon filled with rocks and stone burst open, just as he was passing it. The stones, several tons of them, fell on my Dad, breaking his spine in two places. He died the next day. Because of the misleading evidence given by the pit bosses and a witness, his death was adjudged to be 'by misadventure' and not by accident. My Mum was denied compensation.

At that time the Sunday People offered insurance cover to its regular readers. Death by accident warranted generous compensation, but even though we had proved that we were regular readers they refused to pay up because of the misadventure finding.

After my Dad was killed I spent three years studying mining science, and later another year on a special study of the Coal Mines Act and Regulations and other legislation covering industrial injuries and negligence. After Nationalisation I won the right to become an accident site observer. In doing this work I developed an eagle eye for evidence that would support a claim for compensation.

# A BIT OF LIGHT RELIEF

When I reached the age of 17 and was getting a bit more pocket money, I started to go to the Theatre Royal at Barnsley: up in the Gods at first, but I gradually worked my way to the better seats when I could afford it. I would usually go to the second house on a Saturday. Sometimes I got a mate to go with me, but he wasn't all that interested so I went on my own.

The Theatre turned out at around 11 p.m. and to finish the evening off I would stroll down to the market place where there was a small fair with one or two side shows. On this evening I stopped to listen to a barker, shouting out the attractions of the show. He made great play about the grand finale. "Come in and see Jane and her bare behind!" Jane, a bonny young lass, was on show on the platform, looking very desirable. And the thought of her bare behind raised all kinds of expectations with the men listening. As soon as the barker finished and entry to the show began, the men paid their tanners – sixpences – and trooped in.

For around thirty minutes there were two or three performances: a juggler, a few mystic tricks and what have you. Then came the awaited grand finale. "Laideeze and gentlemen!" the barker bawled, "Here is our beautiful Jane and her bear behind!" Jane danced onto the stage, ever so dainty, and dressed in flesh coloured tights from neck to-toe, holding in her hand behind her a teddy bear. Jane and her bear behind. As the audience left the show there was a bit of good-natured banter. They all knew they had been well and truly "done".

# DRIFTING

In 1939 I got my shot firer's and Deputy's ticket from the Barnsley Technical College. I was offered a job as a pit official, but refused it. I much preferred to keep my job as a development worker driving headings. A heading is a roadway that is driven through solid ground to prepare a coal seam for production. It is the same with drifts: they are roadways that are driven to connect one coal seam to another where they are on different levels. A few years later, because of my experience in driving headings and drifts, the boss persuaded me to become an official so that I could supervise two drifts that were being driven from the beamshaw seam up to the winter seam: two coal seams that were on different levels, with about 130 feet between them. The first drift, which would be the main intake drift and used as the roadway for entrance to the coal face to transport tubs and materials, was at an incline of 1 in 7. The second drift was 200 yards further along the level. This would be the return airway and was cut at a much steeper incline at 1 in 3. It meant that the distance of the drift would be shorter. That meant that, although cutting a drift at this incline is much harder and more dangerous work, it would be less costly.

The strata in coal seams vary. Some strata are of sandstone rock – harder to work, drill and blast, but reasonably safe as a support system. Indeed, when driving through solid rock, supports are hardly needed. The level where I worked as a boy door trapper didn't have a single support all through its length of 1,000 yards. In the beamshaw and winter seams the strata were mostly a grey-blue, clay-like substance. While underground and under pressure this remains rock-hard and will "hold" at the roof and sides, provided it is well supported. But when exposed to the weather and water for any length of time it will disintegrate and become very fragile or even turn into a grey clay-like sludge. Consequently, in these conditions, you have to keep your support system well up to scratch, or there could be a nasty roof fall. Neglect of this factor has cost many a life and limb. My job was to see that the drifts, with the help of the surveyors, were kept straight and in line, at the right incline, width and height, and to make sure that the supports – arched girders, 12 by 8 feet – were set at the correct angle and distance apart, fixed tight to the roof and side, and lined with concrete strips securely placed within the ridges of the girders. I also had to fire the shots.

Three men worked the drift, drilled the holes, shifted the rock and stones, set the girders and extended the provisional air ventilation pipes. In the return drift the work was similar but, because of its steepness, it was much harder and progress was slower. I did have one dispute with the foreman of the drifters. They had set a girder which was two inches out of line and I instructed them to take it out and reset it to the line I had marked on the roof. The following day, when I went in to fire their shots, they had not only refused to reset the girder, but had set another one, also two inches out of line. I refused to fire the shots and told them there would be no more shots fired until the girders had been taken out and reset. The foreman huffed and puffed a bit, so then I had to get a bit tough and tell him he either shifted the bloody girders, at his expense, or I would call in a fresh set of workers to finish the job. His boss, a private contractor, complained to the pit manager, but the manager, on advice from the surveyors, agreed that I was correct upon insisting that the girders be reset.

Eventually the main drift reached the coal face. That meant we could turn right and drive a level towards the return drift. But disaster struck. There was a massive blow-out of gas and work had to be stopped. It is unsafe for men to work where the presence of gas is more than 2%. They had to be withdrawn and arrangements made for an auxiliary fan to be installed at the bottom of the drift to push in extra ventilation and clear the gas. The gas outflow was so severe that the fan had to be kept running 24 hours a day to enable work to continue. All that was easily managed during the week when pit officials were always present in the pit. But during the weekend special arrangements had to be made so that there was always an official in the pit. Rotas were arranged, and I opted for the Sunday afternoon shift – 2 p.m. until 9 p.m.

On the Sunday I write about, I let myself down the pit. There were no banksman or onsettor working – the men responsible for signalling the winding engineman to raise or lower the chair up and down the shaft. So I had to rap my own signals, step smartly into the chair and wait for it to start descending. Getting off the chair at the bottom of the shaft, I would then rap a signal to let the winder know the chair was clear. I was then the only man in the pit. The previous shift man had come out at 1 p.m. to rush off for a pint before the pubs closed.

My first job was to walk along the level to the first drift, examine and start the fan, and then walk up the drift, testing for gas, and examining the ventilation tubes, the roof and sides and supports. Having done that, I would proceed along to the second drift. Because this drift was so steep and the ground so rough, it was always a bit of a tow walking up it. Here I would again test for gas, examine the drift face and the supports.

Having completed my first examination, I would walk back to the pit bottom and into the box office. There I would write up a report, have a cup of tea and a sandwich, and then read the Sunday papers. By this time it would be around 5 p.m. and I would set off on my second examination.

I checked out the fan and the first drift: everything OK. Went along to the second drift and as I walked up it I noticed there was a trickle of water running down the middle of the track. "Must be raining" I thought. I continued up the drift until I got about half way – about 30 yards – and stopped! I looked around at the roof and the supports. Couldn't see anything wrong. Apart from the odd creaks and movements you always notice when the pit is quiet, there was a strange eerie feeling about the place. Everything was still and silent, and I felt distinctly uncomfortable. Weird. I stood looking around, wondering what to do, and then I said to myself, "What the hell's up wi thi, Jooer? Get up the bloody drift."

I set off up, walked 4 or 5 yards, then stopped again. "There's summat wrong," I thought. I looked around nervously. Dead silence. Then I set off like a bat out of hell, scurrying down the drift and into the level. Slowing down, I walked about 30 yards along the level and sat down on some old timbers by the side of the roadway. Sat there for a few minutes, recovered my breath and, feeling calmer, I said to myself, "I shall have to go up and examine the place. But I'll wait a bit first".

Then, all of a sudden, there was a heavy bang, bang, bang! The sound of a thousand thunders, rolling and heaving, for at least a minute. Then everything went still and silent again. I waited, wondering nervously what the hell had happened. Eventually I decided to go and take a look. I walked back, steady and cautious, my spotlight shining ahead of me, so that I could see. And then – full stop! All I could see was a mountain of rock, muck and sludge. The roadway and entrance to the drift were completely blocked. Hundreds of tons of rock, stones and sludge had caved in at the top of the drift and, because it was so steep, crashed with horrendous force down the drift, wrecking and twisting girders and supports, and churning up the sleepers and track.

There was nothing for me to do but go back to the main drift, make a final test for gas, stop the fan and leave the pit. When I got into the lamp room I phoned the manager and made arrangements for a repair team to come in and start muck shifting. It took three teams of four men, working round the clock, five weeks, filling hundreds of tubs of muck, before the real work of making safe the drift, could be started.

Finally the job was finished, but whenever I walked up that drift again I never felt comfortable. What made me panic and gallop down the drift? I don't know.

# MANAGER OR WORKERS' REP?

Completing the drifts and opening up the first coal face ready for manning, I asked the manager if I could have a job as a filler. But he refused me. He wanted me to be the deputy for the face. Reluctantly I agreed, but I was never happy with the job. My instinctive militancy emerged again, and I was soon having disputes with the management about working conditions and safety, and for taking sides with the men when they had a legitimate grievance. The last occasion was when I made an extra payment of £1 each to three men for doing an unpleasant and dangerous job which had to be done if there was to be any coal production the next day. The following Friday, when I came out of the pit, the three men were waiting for me. They told me that the extra allowance I had promised had been taken out by the under-manager.

"Come on then," I said and walked them into the under-manager's office. I demanded to know why an extra payment I had booked for the men had been stopped.

The under-manager, looking down at some papers on his desk, said. "I took it out because I thought you had been a bit too generous. Ten bob should have been enough."

"You weren't there, so how could you know how much the job was worth? It was belting down with rain, it was dangerous and the work had to be done. Nobody wanted to do it, and so John here and his mates agreed, after a lot of persuading, to do the job for an extra quid each. If it hadn't been done there would have been no bloody coal filled next shift."

"Well I think it was too much. I'll pay them ten bob each."

"You bloody well won't," I retorted. And, grabbing him by the collar, "Don't you insult my intelligence by hinting that I don't know my job." And, pulling his head down, I spoke into his ear: "The job had to be done. It was worth more than a pound. I promised them a pound each, and they'll get a bloody pound." Then I let go.

He looked at me, and shouted, "All right! They can have there fucking pound." Then he wrote out a chit for them to collect their money. He also gave me a chit for my cards.

The union got me my job back, but no thanks! By that time I had got another job as a filler at the next pit. There, on my first pay day, I got a bit of a shock. The wages were lower than I expected. After doing a bit of finding out and checking the piece rates I learned that the stints were in line with most pits, but the piece rates were lower than most. At that time, piece rates were negotiated at pit level: the cause of many rag-ups and differences in wages. Grimethorpe and pits around South Yorkshire were mostly militant and enjoyed the best pay rates and better working conditions than most. Rates were low in the pits around Wakefield and West Yorkshire where the union leadership was right-wing, chapelised and docile. Rates in the pit I had joined were almost as bad.

After the initial shock about wages I decided on a programme of re-education for the lads. I talked and talked, sowing discontent amongst them, and explained the difference in pay rates and conditions at other pits. Besides this education programme, whenever any of the lads had a dispute or grievance about his job, safety, or any other matter, I would intervene and take it up with the management. I notched up a few wins and it got so that when a man had a problem, he came to me to help him out.

Gradually I won the trust and support of the men, and built round me a close team of four men that I could depend upon. The management didn't like this. Nor did the local branch officials of the union. Nice talk and nice jobs were offered to me: jobs with little or no work and good wages. It was a common practice in many pits for managements to fix up local union officials with jobs in the airways. Years later, after nationalisation, I remember, when I was negotiating for the men, an Industrial Relations officer from the Yorkshire Division of the National Coal Board said to the manager, "Can't you find Joe a job in the airways?" "No, he bloody can't," I rapped out. A job in the airways meant you went down the pit at 6 a.m., scratted about doing nothing, and then went out of the pit at 8 or 9 a.m. Lots of work-places adopt this practice. Giving a workers' rep something he enjoys and doesn't want to lose is always an effective way of weakening his militancy.

Later the fillers asked me to be the charge-hand for them. It was all grist to the mill for me, and it compelled the management to recognise my authority. A little after a year I had the lads out on strike for a pay-rise, which we won. A year later, and a year after that, we went on strike for further pay rises. By this time we were able to settle down because we were now in the top ten. I had also gotten myself elected as an "accident site observer".

## JONAS

I was working on a double long wall face, and my stint was at the end, across the main gate. This was a ten by eight gate – ten foot wide, and eight foot high – although, as the gate advanced, it got lower as the roof settled down because of the coal being taken out. Up the left hand side of the gate there was a three-foot wide conveyor belt, carrying coal back from the face belts. The tension end of the gate belt was set right up to the face, so that the two face belts, running towards it from either side, could spill coal onto the gate belt. The gate was ripped to within two feet of the face so that a ten-foot split bar (similar to a thick telegraph pole cut into ten-feet lengths) could be set under the rip edge to make safe and to allow the tension end of the gate belt to be put right up to the coal face. On the right hand side of the gate there was a rail track to carry equipment and other materials to the face.

Before going into the face I always examined the rip edge to be sure it was properly supported, and then the roof and sides of the gate. On both sides of the gate, near the rip edge, there were the 'gear-heads': powerful electric motors that drove the belts, encased in thick steel to protect them. Each gear-head was stopped and started by a button man. The right hand gear, which crossed the main gate, was easily accessible to the button man, and he could also watch out for coal getting fast before spilling onto the gate belt. The gear-head on the left hand side was at the back of the gate belt and under the rip edge at the side. All this machinery produced continuous, deafening noise. At the side of the gear-head there was a space about a yard wide between it and the pack side (a pack is a sort of dry wall of stone, packed tight between the roof and the floor which form the side of the gate). In this space, beside the gear-head, the button man would sit to stop and start the belt whenever required.

The man employed at this job was an ex-ripper in his early sixties, past doing heavy work. He was named Jonas, and had been a ripper all his working life, and for many years a main-gate ripper which called for a lot of experience and skill if the job was to be done correctly and safely. Jonas, a nice quiet man and an obedient worker, always did what he was asked to do by the boss. As I examined the side of the gate where he was sat, just under the rip edge, I noticed a large "slip" that was right over his head. A slip is a natural parting between layers of rock, usually running at an angle to the strata. If it is not supported adequately it can be very dangerous. The top layer of rock can slip, crash to the floor, and will sometimes push out any supports that are there.

When I saw the slip and the danger that Jonas was in, I stopped the gate belt, climbed over it and, bending down, shouted through the noise, "Jonas – bring your bloody self out a there!"

"Yer what ?"

"Bring yourself out of there, and quick!" I answered.

Jonas crawled from under the rip edge and asked, "What's up Joey?"

"You've been a ripper all these years. Haven't you seen that bloody slip there?" And, running my hand down the slip, I said, "Look at it! I thought you had more bloody sense than to sit under that lot."

"Well I showed it to the deputy and he said it was alright."

While all this was going on the deputy had been present, but never said a word. I turned to him saying, "What the hell are you playing at? Sending him under there?"

"Well I thought it would be safe enough."

"Safe my arse – you know its not safe!"

"Well how are we going to stop the belt then?"

"Use the bloody panel!"

"But I'll have to send for a spare man to shout to Jonas if he's at the panel."

"Well get a spare man, unless you want to go under."

The deputy turned to the other button man and said. "Jack Adams is at the top of the gate doing some repairs. Go up and tell him to come down here." Then Jack Adams, the overman and the undermanager all came hurrying down. "What's up now? What do you want a spare man for?" The deputy, explaining what had happened, said, "Joey here won't let Jonas go into the packhole" (the place where Jonas had been sitting). "He's having to start and stop the belt from the panel." (The panel is a transformer where the cables from the headgears and the coal cutters are plugged in. They each have a switch where the power can be turned off or on. Every month they are moved down to the face as it advances, so that they are not too far away.) The overman, a weasel-faced runt and a religious maniac, was the biggest lying twister in the pit. He sneered, "You want to get some iron jelloids; I can't see owt wrong with the place."

"Then you bloody well get under there."

"It's not my job" he replied, and then shouted up to Jonas, "Jonas!

Come down here and get under there and start the belt." Jonas made to climb over the belt.

"Jonas!" I shouted sharply, "Don't be such a bloody fool! You're not going under there. Get back to the panel!"

The undermanager then intervened, "I don't see anything wrong with it, Joe."

"Well you wouldn't, would you? For the sake of a couple of quid, you'd put a man's life at risk." And a bit of an argument began, and then: shweeze! there was a crack and then a scraping noise as the slip slipped. A block of razor edged rock, three feet wide, four feet thick and about seven feet long, slithered to the floor, right where Jonas would have been sitting.

"Now," I said to the undermanager, "What a pity you and that runt are not under it."

A week or two later I was sat in the club and Jonas came to sit beside me, bringing me a pint. "Do you know, Joey, I have a confession to make. I've never disliked you, but I've always thought of you as an agitator, always looking for trouble. But me and my wife thank God there are blokes like you about. We'll never be able to thank you enough for what you did that morning."

## PUTNEY ROYAL HOSPITAL FOR INCURABLES

There were times when I used to walk round the house feeling restless and unsettled. My family had learned from experience that I was sort of gearing myself up to take a long trip on my bike. The buzz word within my family was that I suffered from wanderlust, and they were reading the signs that I was ready for the 'off'.

It happened every spring time or early summer. I wanted to be away, on the road; to be free. Every year I would pack a few essentials and be ready to go wherever my bike took me. This year, 1934 when I was nineteen, I was up at around 5 a.m. I knew that I was ready for going that morning. I got washed and dressed, packed a few belongings, checked and oiled my bike. I stood looking around for a few minutes and then I went upstairs, as I always did, looked quietly into the bedrooms and whispered my dear good mornings and then I was away. My trips used to vary in distance and time. Sometimes I was away for a couple or three weeks; sometimes longer.

The longest time I was away was when I packed in my job as a trammer, collected my cards and went to work in Slough. At other times I never asked for my cards. I never told my mates or the boss that I was leaving and wouldn't know when I would be back. Like most miners, I was hung up on the job, used to revel in the challenge of it, but hated the unnecessary harsh conditions of it. The odd thing about it was that although I was away from the pit I was always still doing the work. New ideas and a fresh approach to the job would occupy my mind, and eventually I would become restless to get back to it. With hindsight, I would say I was coming to realise the benefits of what we now call the sabbatical.

In 1934 I had two spells away. On the first trip, I biked down the A1. We knew it as the Great North Road. I headed south, not knowing where I was going but just following my instincts. I turned off the A1 and headed west, still not knowing where I was. By mid evening I noticed I was on the road to Hitchin. Then I pulled up at a pub, all lit up, bright and inviting. I had a pint and a bite, sat ruminating for a while, then decided to go a bit further. Along the road there was a river and, beside it, a nice green field. By the hedgerow there was a haystack and I decided that, because it was such a lovely evening, the haystack would be my bed for the night. If the weather was good I usually slept out; if not, then I would look for a cheap bed and breakfast, usually at roadside cafés.

I was up early next morning, before 6. I got my towel and things, walked across to the river, stripped off and had a vitalising swim. Then I washed, shaved and set off on my journey. Two or three miles down the road, I pulled up at a small roadside café, mostly used by lorry drivers, where I enjoyed myself a bit of breakfast – egg, bacon, beans and toast, and lashings of bread and marge. Then I went to sit on an easy chair beside the window, and browsed through yesterday's paper.

An advertisement caught my eye. It invited applications for the post of male nurse – "no experience necessary" – in the Royal Hospital for Incurables at Putney, London. Aye, I thought, I'll try that. My only relevant qualification was a certificate for massage and physiotherapy which I had got through the SAME Institute at Leatherhead. So, I thought, I'll have another cuppa and be on my way.

It was a beautiful sunny morning, always the best and freshest part of the day – even more so if you are free to be out and to rejoice in the bliss of it all. Whizzing down the road on this beautiful sunny morning, I felt so happy, free and full of energy, my spirits were mountains high. It was as near to perfect joy and freedom as I could ever dream of.

I arrived at Putney around lunch time and found my way to the hospital. I rode through some tall iron gates, along a circular drive, parked my bike and walked into the receptionist's office. I asked to see the Matron, and said why I had called. After a wait of ten minutes, I was taken to the Matron's office. I took one good look at her, and what I saw was not a happy sight. She looked a very daunting woman: tall, angular and with the aura, looks and bearing of the toughest Regimental Sergeant Major you would never wish to meet. She had been a matron in a wartime military hospital in France during the '14-18 war. It seemed she was short of nurses, and we agreed that I would start work there at once. All male nurses had to live in. Room and board were provided, and a salary of 15 shillings a week. I was installed in a sparse but comfortable room, and then kitted up with a uniform – white trousers, white cap, white shoes and unlined jackets with narrow blue and white stripes, plus a few other bits and pieces.

I was able to have a spot of lunch and then went into a room, along with three other nurses, and given two hours of rudimentary training. How to look after the patients; how to lift them, turn them, wash and bathe them. Then I was taken to a ward where there were four patients. They were to be my regular patients and I was responsible for their care. A sister, another sergeant major type, went through the motions of introducing me to them. Not that they could understand much of what she was saying. She talked down to them in a sickeningly patronising manner. There was no tenderness in her voice or her manner. Ice-cold indifference it seemed. I didn't like it one bit and already could feel my hackles rising.

The patients were ex-service men, once fine young men who had been badly damaged during their service in the front line. They were not really old, but they looked old, very old, some of them almost to the point of dementia. They were not men, just bodies, fragile bones covered with bleach-white skin stretched tightly over them as though it was a material in short supply. Their bodies, their senses, had been smashed by whatever injuries and ordeals they had suffered. They were unable to communicate except by the odd tortured word, or an attempt to use some form of sign language. I learned that it was only by their facial expressions and the pained look in their eyes that I was able to reach some semblance of closeness towards them. Their bodily movements were severely restricted and, if they did manage to move a limb, that was achieved in pain and anguish. Maybe a hand could hold your finger after the manner a baby does when looking for security. They lay in their beds for most of the day, but were sometimes dumped in a chair for the odd hour, or if you wanted to change the bed. Just mindless lumps of bone, skin and a bit of flesh here and there, they were of no weight at all, easy to lift and carry.

My first job was to get them up at 6 in the morning, wash and bathe them, shave them, then change their clothing and soiled sheets. Then I would massage their frail limbs and backs, and ever so gently treat their bed sores. I did my very best to make them comfortable if that was possible. Then I would fetch their breakfast and feed them.

It was heart breaking, tear-jerking work, and, although it could not be said to be pleasant, I felt honoured to be able to do what I could for them. It was a new, different, sad world I had entered. But I felt disturbed and angry because of the almost callous disregard the staff often displayed for these once proud and strong young men. It was unbelievable that they seemed so unaffected by the misery of it. Already, by the second day, I was having disputations with the staff about their indifference towards these men. "You'll soon get used to it," they remarked, and I shuddered at the thought of that. These sad men were never seen as once proud fighting soldiers, paying a horrible price for their duty to "King and Country". They were looked upon as something in a vegetable plot that had gone to seed; or as animals in a zoo. I soon learned what was meant by being case-hardened – a condition only too prevalent among professionals engaged for too long in one particular branch of a caring profession.

Regardless of the pain and sadness of the work, I was happy to stay with it. It was hard, the hours were long, but I would give it a go! One of the men had been a Colonel. I looked at him humbly. How could it be that this wreck of a body that I was washing – this once fine, intelligent soldier, the victim of the folly and greed of ambitious politicians – was now reduced to a shivering assembly of bone and skin. It seemed to me that patience, kindness, veracity, humility and love should be the most important qualities of caring work, and should be the most important part of the training for those who do this work. But I could see very little sign of them here. And from what I have witnessed, and from what my wife and others have told me, things have not changed much today.

"Do not get involved" was what they taught us as trainees; aye, and for those already employed, cost or convenience took precedence over care. Well if carers are not to become involved with their patients or clients, how can they do their jobs? In my work, when helping or advising people, I have always felt it essential to become "involved" with them. That's the only effective way to understand their problems and to find solutions or bring comfort. But to do the job as it should be done may call for more staff and more money, and that the tax payers may not want to provide. Not unless, by some unfortunate mischance, they have members of their own families in need of care. Then their perspective changes.

Anyway, I decided to stick with the job. At one o'clock we knocked off for lunch, and then we were free until four. During my two hours break I would rest on my bed for an hour. There was a games room and a small gym provided for the nurses. Some of the nurses played snooker or whatever. But I preferred to use the gym. I would have a good workout, a shower and a vigorous rub down, and be ready at 4 o'clock to go out to my patients again.

There was always one or more of them in need of attention, even if it was only just a bit of loving care and some comforting. At six, I would bed them down for the long night. What happened after that, God only knows, because every morning, one or more of them were in a right mess: pyjamas and bedding soaked in urine and coated with excreta. The men, to add to their handicaps, were clearly emotionally disturbed. As I approached them, they would shrink back, whimpering and fearful of what might happen to them. I was ashamed, sad and angry. Why should they appear to be so afraid? They were here for care, nursing, compassion and love. Instead they were shut away – out of sight, out of mind: forlorn and unforgiven for the trouble they were. No emergency bells for them in these grim workhouse-type wards. They were inmates, dependent upon charity for their keep and custody. Some of the men had medals for bravery. What I witnessed now was the best an ungrateful "King and Country" would do for them – a price more destructive than the ultimate sacrifice so many of their comrades made.

The long hours and low pay didn't bother me, but it did explain why the labour turnover was so high. There were other more easily avoidable reasons as well in the arrogance of the matron and senior sisters towards the nursing staff. They treated their untrained male nurses as if they should be doing penance for some past failure.

I completed my first week at the hospital and on my eighth day, after breakfast, I approached the matron and asked her about the weekly day off I had been promised.

"Yes," she said. "You get a day off after every seventh working day."

"In that case, today should be my day off," I said.

"Yes, it's your day off today".

"But I've been on duty this morning, until lunch…"

"That's right," the matron interrupted. "Your day off starts after lunch. You get extra time off when you have been here a year."

I was flabbergasted! What a neat piece of trickery; and I let her know my feelings in no uncertain terms. When I left the matron to go back to the ward, my blood was boiling. But I soon cooled off as I tended to the comfort and consolation of those poor unfortunate men. As I wiped off the slaver and spit from the face of one man, I looked into his eyes, the window of his soul. Is there something there? I wondered. Could I detect a look of recognition, of gratefulness? My heart melted. There was such a great need for love for these fragments of men. Not pity, that would be wrong: humility and love, and I tried my best to provide them.

I finished my work at one o'clock and then went for lunch and to begin my day off. I followed my usual routine, relaxation for one hour and then a workout and shower in the gym. The workout and the shower was the one good part of the day that I really enjoyed. Supper wasn't until 6 o'clock so I skipped that to get a look around Putney. I strolled around for a while, didn't much care for what I saw, and so went into the pictures. I think it was a good film, but I didn't much notice it. My mind was too taken up with the events of the past week and the shock to my system. I grieved for the men and their conditions. But how could

I change things? Nobody wanted to listen. I was just a bit of driftwood at the mercy of the tide.

I came out of the pictures, my mind in a muddle. I was missing the comradeship of my old Barnsley mates and felt I could never get to like these stuck-up southerners anyway. I strolled around for a while, and then thought I would try a drop of the local brew. I went into a pub and ordered a pint of their best bitter. The barman pulled a pint and put it on the bar. I looked at it. It looked as flat as a fart. No top on it at all. And it tasted even worse. I was expecting the fresh tang and flavour of good old Barnsley Bitter. I took a drink, and nearly threw up. "Christ" I said, "It tastes like witch-piss."

The barman looked at me, saying, "What's wrong?"

"This" I said, "It tastes rotten."

"I can't see anything wrong with it," said the barman.

"Well I'm not supping that. It tastes like poison."

"You're from the North aren't you?"

"Aye," I said, "I'm from Barnsley, and we sup good beer up there, not this muck."

"You're always grumbling, you lot," scowled the barman.

"I should bloody well think so. Call that beer?" I said haughtily. "Well if you don't like it, get out," the barman sneered. And with a very hasty response, I scoffed, "Dunt worry. I'm not supping that piss."

I then tried another pub, another brew, but it wasn't much better. The time was now half past nine, so I decided to go back to the Bastille. The big iron gates were closed, and locked. I pressed a bell-button and a bloke came out of a close-by hut.

"What do you want?" he asked.

"I want to come in. I work here."

"Well nobody is allowed in after nine, unless they have a pass. What's your name?"

He then went into the hut, and made a 'phone call. Then he came out and opened the gates.

"You have to see the matron at ten in the morning," he said

I was up at 5.30 the next morning as usual, and just before six I went to my ward to attend to my patients. Then at 10 I kept my appointment with old flint-heart. As soon as I got through the door, she laid into me as though I was some sort of criminal being carpeted for some heinous offence.

"Who do you think you are?" she bellowed across the parade ground. "House rules lay it down that no one shall be out after 9 p.m. unless they have permission to be so."

Well, that's it, I thought. I had felt in my bones that before long there would be a shoot-out between us. I had taken more than I was prepared to tolerate, and so I let her have it. With both guns blazing.

"When it is my day off, madam, I will go, and I will come, as I please. It is my time, and I will use it as I wish." And then I let her know what I thought about the treatment she was dishing out to the patients and the nurses.

"Anyone with bollocks will not put up with this," I said, politely.

"You'll be in for nine o'clock or you will be fined a day's pay," she cried.

"Not likely, mate," I snorted. "There will be no fines, no penalties. I'll do my job best I can, but I'm not putting up with your tantrums, in my time!"

"Any more of that, and you will be on a month's notice," she bawled.

"There will be no notice, missy. I'm finished. I'm off, pronto, just as soon as I have packed my bags."

The matron stood up, and with great pomp and haughtiness said,

"You cannot leave until you have served a month's notice."

I just gave her a sweet smile and left.

I walked round to my room, packed my few things, got out my bike from the shed, then rode down to the prison gates. They were shut and locked. The gateman was there to bar me. I looked at him, weighing him up. Not much resistance there, I thought. Then speaking softly to him, I said, "Look mate, I'm normally a peace loving man. I don't like bother." Then, raising my voice, I said, sharply, "If you don't open that gate now, I'll bloody well knock you through it."

"I'm sorry, Sir", he said, apologetically, "but my orders are not to let you out."

He then realised that I had a thumb lock on the back of his right hand. It needed only slight pressure to make him bend and cause him some pain. "Look," I said. "I'll help you. Give me the keys and I'll open the gates for you." He gave me the keys.

As I peddled off on my bike I felt guilty about deserting those poor souls I had left behind. But my bridges were down. There was no going back. Many times, since then, I have thought about them and that horrible world they lived in. And I have often wondered if there are other similar, hidden worlds. I have an uneasy feeling that there are.

## GEARHEADS – FIRE HAZARD

Shortly after the incident with Jonas the face hit the colliery boundary and had to close. We were transferred to a new face. This time I moved back to my old stint as a corner man. The corner was the end part of the face. It was a shorter stint because some of the coal had to be handled twice because the face stretched a couple of yards beyond the belt. It also had to be trimmed so that the coal cutter could be "stabled" there. That gave me time to go through the face to check with the lads that everything was okay.

On this day it was getting near shift time and the lads had nearly filled off, lifting maybe a couple of yards of coal each. Then I sniffed up and thought there must be summat burning. I sniffed again, and yes, I could smell rubber burning. I shouted to my mate, Charly, in the next stint, "Can you smell owt burning Charly?"

"Aye, it smells like rubber."

The smell was getting stronger as I lay on the belt and rode up the face on it to the gear-head and the main gate. As I got nearer to the gear-head, the smell got very much worse and I could feel the heat coming from the gear-head. I got to the gate, scrambled through the belt and banged down hard on the stop button. The Deputy was sat there, showing no concern at all, and as I stopped the belt, he cried, "Whats tha done that for?"

"Can't you smell the bloody gear, you pillock? It's bloody burning!"

"I can't smell owt."

"No you fucking wouldn't, would you? The gear is so hot it's a wonder it hasn't blown the fucking pit up, you half-gotten git!"

"Well can it run for the rest of the hour. They've nearly filled off."

"No it can't fucking run, and its bloody well not going to." I was so boiling with anger, I called the deputy all the pit names I could lay my tongue to.

"Well what can we do then?" asked the deputy, by now rather subdued.

"Tell the men to gob their coal" – meaning pile it in the mouth of the gate.

Then the deputy said, "I'd better go up to the 'phone and tell the undermanager."

Knowing that if the men left the face before shift time, without filling off, they could lose wages, I sent a message down the face for them to release the tension end of the belt (this would slacken it and prevent it from running) and to gob their coal and timber up. I then walked up 30 yards to the transformer panel and disconnected the gear-head from the power by taking out the pummel (the pummel was what you might call a sort of plug, ten inches long and four inches in diameter, brass lined and connected to an armoured cable reaching down to the gear-head). When the pummel was withdrawn, the power was completely cut off and the gear-head could not be started either deliberately or accidentally.

Twenty minutes later, the undermanager came steaming down, all lathered up and sweating profusely.

"What the fucking hell's wrong now, Kenyon?" he bawled.

"The gear-head is over-heating. It's too hot to handle and too dangerous to start."

"Well it's going to fucking start. I want that face filling off – it'll only take them twenty minutes."

"They'll soon be filled off" I said. "I've told them to gob it."

"Well you've got no fucking right to. They won't get paid, I'll tell you that much."

Then the undermanager, 'Greeny' as we knew him, shouted down the face:

"Don't gob the coal! We're going to start the belt."

I sat there blandly watching Greeny scrabble off and hit the starting button. Nothing happened. "For Christ's sake, what's wrong now?" he howled out, on the verge of throwing a fit.

I looked and grinned. The poor sod, I thought. For the sake of a couple of tons of coal he'll put himself in that condition. Then the deputy meekly said,

"He's taken the pummel out mister."

"You've no authority to do that Kenyon," he bawled.

"I've got all the authority I need."

"And where do you get that from?" he shouted.

Looking at Greeny benignly, for I was enjoying this, I said sweetly, "Safety, my dear. Safety."

I thought he was going to blow a gasket. Greeny then hurried to the transformer with the intention of putting the power back on. On our way to the transformer, I picked up a two feet six inch pit prop. And as Greeny bent down to pick up the pummel I held the pit prop above his hand and, with menace, said "You touch that pummel mate, and I'll stick your bleeding fingers to it."

Greeny again made to pick up the pummel — and wallop! I brought down the prop sharply onto the pummel. "Now let that be a warning. Keep off!"

Greeny then turned to the overman, who had by now joined him. "You heard that, didn't you? I'm having him in Court for threatening me with violence."

An electrician had been sent for and, at this moment, he came hurrying down. Greeny told him to examine the gear-head and to let him know if it could be started. The electrician scrabbled into the face, then shouted, "Sorry; I can't examine the gear-head. It's too hot."

"Well how long will it be before you can examine it?" Asked Greeny.

"Can't say," replied the electrician.

"Then can we start the belt then?"

"I wouldn't advise it. I think you should send for the chief electrician." Half an hour later the chief electrician arrived. He went onto the face and by this time the gear-head had cooled sufficiently for him to get a spanner on and take off one of its side plates. "Good God!" he exclaimed, "The motor's melting — can't understand how it run as long as it did. Look at the cables; the rubber protection has melted off and exposed all the wiring. It's a good job you cut the power off. You could have had a fire, or even blown the place up ..." Then he continued, "I'm afraid this engine is finished. It will have to go out of the pit while a new one's brought down."

I looked at Greeny and — just to rub it in — I said, "You'll be taking me to court then?"

Greeny scowled and said nowt.

# IRENE

After my trip to Putney I went back to my job at the pit, but the pits went on short time soon afterwards. It was a regular practice in the summer months, when demand for coal fell, for the pits to go on to a three-day week. Coal production was at that time worked out on a regional basis and a pit basis so that work was shared out and pit closures were avoided. It's easy to close and reopen a factory, but you can't do that with a pit. At these times ours used to work on Monday, Tuesday and Thursday.

When the lads came out of the pit on a Tuesday or Thursday they would eagerly look at the notice board in the pit yard for the message "No work tomorrow". Men with families were a bit concerned about it because they needed the money, although many of them welcomed the rest it gave them. They would, however, get three days' unemployment pay. But the single lads were quite chuffed. For them it meant freedom to be away and do whatever they fancied to do. My mates sometimes biked off to the fields between Barnsley and Wakefield, pulling peas. They were paid ninepence for each 40-pound bag. They didn't earn a lot because they were not serious pullers and they larked around a good deal, but they enjoyed the fresh air and earned enough to buy a packet of fags and go to the pictures. Sometimes, but not very often, I went to the fields, but because I never smoked I would put a pound of raisins from the Co-op in my pocket and buy with my earnings a slab of fruit cake for the family. The raisins I carried around in my jacket, having a munch now and again. Most of my spare time was spent at a lake known as Woolley Dam, four miles from our home. It was a place lots of people visited, to swim, fish, go boating, or just sit and watch their kids splash around in the shallows, and it was my favourite haunt. I almost lived there at holiday times, swimming or boating or helping with the boats. Indeed, I was such a regular visitor, the owners got to know me very well and gave me free access to the place. They also loaned me a twelve-foot skiff for my own use. It was a slim, sleek, fast little craft, with just the one seat for the rower. They let me use it because while I was there I helped to fetch in boats that were overdue or had been left abandoned on the far side of the lake.

The skiff was beautiful and, whether I rowed or paddled it, would skim over the water like a bird. Rowers who had gone over their time and were awkward about coming in soon changed their minds when I gave their boat a gentle nudge with the skiff and a promise of a more severe ram if they didn't move. Because of the many hours I spent there, wearing only swimming trunks, I developed a wonderful shiny tan over my body. I also avoided white blobs in the covered areas by rowing and swimming in the nude when no-one else was there.

During the late 1920s and throughout the 1930s Woolley Dam was always my favourite place. Along with other kids, during the school holidays and on Saturday mornings, we would walk the four miles to the Dam, splash around in the water, walk along the weir, and play among the trees in nearby woods and climb them. We picked bluebells, dog daisies, nuts, conkers and blackberries. But there is one beautiful, everlasting memory that I shall always associate with this lovely place.

It was during the war, in 1941, that I got a weekend's leave. Walking down the street to catch the train back to my unit, I saw this stunning girl getting on a bus with her sister. They were going to the pictures. We looked at each other and smiled, and in two seconds she was gone, with no chance to exchange a word. But I had fallen deeply in love.

I cursed myself for not getting on the bus with her. From that moment and for the year afterwards I dreamed about her, talked to her in my imagination and wondered how I could find her. I learnt that her name was Irene, and every time I got any leave I searched for her, but without any luck. And then one evening, on Friday 25 July, 1942, God smiled upon me. I walked into this small village pub, the Fox and Hounds, near where I thought she lived, and as I walked into the pub, who should I see but her sister, sitting with their Ma. I asked if I could sit at their table and buy them a drink. Then I asked Annie, their Ma, how Irene was. She told me that Irene was living in Doncaster with her sister Gladys. She had gone there to work in a tank factory. My heart sank. But then – wow! – she told me that Irene would be home tomorrow evening, Saturday.

I walked on air, all three miles home. Saturday morning came, and the day dragged by, waiting for the time to get the bus to the Fox. But eventually I got there, full of fears that she might not come. But there she was, looking radiantly beautiful. I could sense that she had gone to great lengths to present herself at her absolute best; and she had saved me a chair beside her. I looked into her eyes and there is just no way I can describe how happy I felt. How could such a beautiful being be interested in me? And then, without thinking, I moved my head close to hers and said, "Will you marry me?" She straightened up and laughed, saying, "That's a new technique."

"No", I said urgently. "I love you, and I want to marry you." She smiled, but didn't say yes or no. Then she held my hand and said, "I like you very much, but I hardly know you."

I spent the whole wonderful evening with her. And later, before we said our final good night, I asked if she would spend tomorrow with me at Woolley Dam. "Hm, I'd love to" she said. I told her it was my birthday tomorrow and she laughed ever so sweetly, saying, "You're a right romantic, aren't you? The first words you ever say to me are 'will you marry me?' And now you tell me it's your birthday tomorrow."

"Come to Woolley with me, and it will be the best birthday present I've ever had." And it was.

First we sat on the grass together, holding hands, talking and getting to know each other better, growing closer by the minute. Then I asked her to go out in a boat with me. I would take her round the lake, show her my favourite swimming spot, and the little secret coves that I knew of. As I helped her on to the boat she clung tightly to me, our eyes met, and I knew that we loved each other. I rowed around the lake and pulled the boat under the shade of a large tree, beside the water. We sat together and talked and I made her laugh, and I felt that we were getting closer. Then I asked her for her hanky and, knotting the corner of it to the corner of mine, I set them to tether the boat to the tree. I said to her, quietly and tenderly, "We have tied the knot, and we are now anchored together as husband and wife for ever." Then we had our first long embrace and drifted heavenly through a long, long, blissful kiss. We were truly bound together from that moment. As I looked into her eyes, I said to her tenderly, "If I get a house, will you come and live with me? Straight away?"

"Yes I will love" she said and hugged me tightly.

We spent all that marvellous Sunday together, and half the night. It was early next morning, Monday, before we finally tore ourselves apart. Irene was supposed to be back at Doncaster already, and I should have been back at my station too. I was employed by the Ministry of Aircraft Production on security work, where they were making and testing Radar. I managed to get an early train to Manchester and then on to the place where I was stationed, having already 'phoned them to say that I had been delayed and would be a couple of hours late.

Later I scoured the local papers, looking for a house to let. "Not much choice today" said the boss, who had been helping with the search. Next day I searched again and "bingo!" I spotted one. "Semi-detached furnished house, for rent." I took an instant hour off and belted away to look at it. When I got there I learned, much to my sorrow, that the woman who owned the house had just let it to another man who was coming to work in the area. However, for consolation, I was invited in and offered a cup of tea. We sat and talked for a while, and before long we became quite friendly. Then, after a second cuppa, she suddenly said, "You can have the house. I'll cancel the other man. When do you want to move in?"

Wow! What joy; "If next Saturday is OK with you," I said, "I would like to move in then."

"That's fine," she said, and I became a householder.

Bursting with energy and ever so happy, I rushed back to work and sent an immediate wire to Irene. "Got a house coming Friday to fetch you love Joe." Then I wrote her a letter, giving her my 'phone number and asking her to call me. She 'phoned Wednesday evening from a call box so I took her number, called her back and we had a nice long talk. She was longing to come to me, and could hardly wait for Friday. Then, on Thursday evening, she phoned me again. "Don't come to Doncaster," she said – my heart stopped; she's changed her mind, I thought – "But come to Barnsley". What a relief! Then she explained that her Ma wanted to have a talk with me. "But don't worry love. I shall be coming with you." Later I learned that Irene had been in torment all week, wondering how she could tell her Mum she was running off with this man she had fallen in love with.

After what seemed like a year, Friday came. As soon as my work was done I galloped off to Manchester to catch a train to Barnsley. But that train, already delayed, soon came to a halt. My stomach churned with anxiety. It was now running an hour late and I wanted to get out and push it. I just couldn't sit still. Would she wait for me? Eventually we got to Barnsley. I was off the train before it stopped, rushed madly to the bus station, and then had another wait for the bus to Shafton where Irene lived. Demons were devouring my innards. When will this lousy bus come? My dear Irene was in despair as well. She had paced up and down, in and out of the house, watching and waiting for every bus from town. But I did arrive and there – joy of joys – she was waiting for me. I stumbled off the bus into her arms.

Irene took me home and her Ma made me a nice cup of tea, although she had given me up for lost. She said that she wanted to have a good talk, and she was quite frank – said she had tried to talk Irene out of coming with me but had failed to get through to her. Gladys, Irene's sister, had come over from Doncaster with Irene so that she could see me, and she turned to her Ma, saying "It's no good going on about it Mum. I've tried talking to her, but she just won't listen. So you had better make the best of it."

I sat down to enjoy a very nice tea and thanked Annie for it. "Well; it's very good of you lad," she said, "but our Rene's made it all."

Gradually we all became very pally, much to Irene's relief. Annie confided in me that she liked me very much, and hoped I would make Irene very happy. Then we all went out for a drink together, and came home for supper and more talk. It was a happy evening. But Saturday morning was on my mind and I was impatient for it to come. Eventually Ma said it was time we were all in bed. She saw Gladys and Irene off, and I felt a bit disappointed because I was hoping for a quick cuddle before we had to say goodnight. I was sleeping on the sofa, for Ma was determined to protect Irene right up to the last. Before she went up to bed though, she gave me a gentle peck on the cheek saying, "You will look after her for me Joe, won't you?"

"Yes Ma, I will, I swear". And we said goodnight.

Saturday came at last, and Gladys and Ma came with us to Barnsley to see us off on the train to Manchester and beyond. We had started on our long, long journey through life together. It was wonderful. We married some months later, in November, but July 27 was always our celebration day: the day, every year, when we exchanged anniversary cards expressing our love for each other. I still have the very last one she sent, on July 27, 1996, the year she died. It says: "Happy Anniversary to my Joe from your Irene. I love you – forever." [7]

# HARRY DIXON

Back to the pits after the war and more stories come to mind. It was about 9 a.m. and I had just about filled half my stint when I got a message telling me to go to 3 north. The main-gate rip – the entry to the coal face there – had collapsed and Harry Dixon was buried beneath it. I quickly put on my clothes and hurried to 3 north about 500 yards away. When I got there they had just exposed Harry. He was moaning and in great pain. The deputy gave him a shot of morphine, and arranged for a stretcher to be brought up close to him. He suspected that Harry's back might be broken and that there were other fractures. The job of getting Harry from under the rip edge and out of danger called for intense care and delicacy. In such situations, although speed might be essential, gentle, easy movement of the patient had to be the rule.

They got on with the job of looking after Harry, but my job was to examine the site of the accident and to look for the cause. Harry was suffering and likely to be disabled – and he deserved compensation. Accidents don't happen, they are caused, and it was for me to find that cause. First, I saw that there was a gate roof support missing at the rip edge. The support under the rip edge was fractured and had been pushed out by the force of the collapse. When I examined the support I discovered that it was old timber, dry and cracked because of constant use, and indeed unfit to be a roof support. It had been used because there was no other timber available. Indeed, it had been used for the past three shifts and had suffered the force of three explosions when the gate had been drilled and blasted to advance the roadway. No wonder it had given way and allowed the roof to collapse.

There had been negligence on the part of the rippers who should have refused to do the job; and of the pit officials in forcing them to do the job and to work with unsafe materials. They had also been negligent in failing to have adequate supports readily available. It didn't call for much ingenuity to prove that Harry's injuries had been caused by wilful, even criminal, negligence. Added to all that, when I examined the rip face, there was enough evidence to show that it had been fractured and weakened by previous rips. This would have been caused by the shot-firer using charges that were too strong for the job, or because the holes had been drilled a little too far into the rock face, fracturing the ripping beyond the depth it should have been. An added cause would be because the rippers had not trimmed the rip face sufficiently to make it safe for supporting. I've seen it happen many a time. Indeed, when I worked across the main gate in the previous face I refused on several occasions to start work until the rip edge had been trimmed, loose rock and stones pulled down, and fresh supports set under the rip edge – always to the great annoyance of the deputy and other pit officials.

Harry, and he's not alone, paid heavily for somebody's negligence. It is a deputy's statutory duty to make sure that all working places are made safe, but far too often fear of the boss and greed for production take priority over the safety of the worker.

Having noted all the evidence, I wrote it down in my diary which I always carried at work. Then, when Harry had been made ready for carrying away on the stretcher – and still in great pain – I got the witnesses to sign the statement I had prepared. I had learned from experience that it is absolutely vital to get signatures from witnesses on the spot, while the victim is present. Far too often, union reps wait days or even weeks before they get statements from witnesses. By this time it is too late. Witnesses may have been got at, it becomes difficult for them to remember exactly what happened and they are reluctant to sign statements. Local union reps often lack the skill and training to root out the cause of an accident. Union HQs can only operate successfully if they are provided with the right kind of evidence to prosecute for damages. That evidence has to come mainly from the local union rep.

Many workers are not protected by having a union rep at their place of work. Even when they are present, they often lack the training and the skill to examine an accident site. There is a statutory Health and Safety Executive, but unless there is patently obvious negligence and a large-scale disaster they are about as effective as a gelding at a stud farm. They are useless when it comes to the "ordinary" accidents which leave so many workers crippled for life. The job of the union is not just to negotiate wages and hours of work. It has an even greater duty to protect its members from injuries at work and, where injury is caused, to be effective in fighting for compensation for the loss and injury suffered.

# ACCIDENTS DON'T HAPPEN

It was shift time; I had filled off and, with my mates, came off the coal-face to get dressed for home. Then I heard a voice shout, "Joe, you're wanted! Bob Harris has had his face smashed in!"

I went back onto the face and there, beside the belt, Bob was lying and groaning, blood all over the place. He had gone into the face-corner to release the tension end of the broad belt that carries the coal back from the face, to slacken the belt so that it could be dismantled and rolled up to make way for the coal-cutter to come through. To do this he had to release two sylvesters which held back the return drum of the belt. He pulled back on the first to ease off the drum and, crash! the sylvester handle whip-lashed from the sword and hit him a mighty blow in the face. His nose and jaw were broken and there was a two-inch hole in his face. I looked at him, then turned to the lads and sent them off for a stretcher and the deputy. I comforted Bob the best way I could, and as soon as he was on the stretcher and on the way out of the pit I started searching around for the cause of the accident.

I examined the sylvester for any defects, and saw that the nut and the bolt, used to anchor the handle to the sword, was missing. I scratched around the immediate area but couldn't find them. Then I made a minute search of the dust and coal dirt, and there it was – the cause of the accident: a steel road nail, used for nailing rail-tracks to their wooden sleepers, three inches long and 5/8 of an inch in diameter. The nail had been used in place of the bolt which should have been doing the job. It had been in there for the last couple of shifts and, because of the strain of holding the belt tight, it had bent and slipped out of its anchor, allowing the handle to fly out. Poor old Bob had got the full weight of it, right in his face.

By this time the deputy came onto the face. I showed him the nail, and he did his own search for the bolt but couldn't find it. Then, in order to save his own skin and much to my delight, he told me that he had reported this defect yesterday. He thought the fitter had repaired it. That made a clear case of negligence, and Bob duly collected adequate compensation to cover his loss of wages plus.

In spite of improved standards of safety at work, the disabilities caused by injuries at work did not abate. The miners won the right to have Coal Mines Inspectors, but they were largely ineffective because there were too many pits and not enough inspectors. I enjoyed a visit from one of these inspectors. We were having difficulties about timber shortages. Some of the men had told me that they were having to come off the face and look for pit props, or set old ones that were not suitable. Having all this in mind, I was walking across the pit yard and learned that the pit inspector was in the managers' office. It was a fine, sunny afternoon and the door of the office was ajar. So I walked in and, much to the embarrassment of the manager and the group manager, who was also present, I naively blurted out the complaints men were making about being short of face timber. The inspector bobbed his head round the door and said, "What's that you say lad?"

Looking at the manager with feigned apology – although, he knew what I was playing at – I explained to the inspector that the lads had made several complaints about the shortage of face timber, and they were having to scour the gates looking for props. It was beautiful to watch the contortions the management went through – but very effective, because next shift there was more bloody timber stacked around the gates than you would find in the Amazonian rain forests.

Things don't always go so well. A filler was in the pit baths, built for us after nationalisation. Getting ready to go down the pit, he stripped off, put his clothes in the clean locker, and went round to the dirty lockers to put on his pit rags. Then he remembered that he had forgotten his chewing tobacco. He hurried back to get it and, on the way, he slipped on the wet floor and broke his leg. Although the pit baths were part of his "sphere of employment" he lost his claim for industrial injury benefit because it was adjudged that having chewing tobacco at work is not incidental to his employment. Had he been going back for his soap, it would have been a different matter. Having soap to shower with after work is incidental to his employment.

A ripper on his way out of the baths slipped on the steps and broke his arm and collar-bone. His claim was disallowed, too. Before reaching the steps leading out of the pit baths, he had called into the canteen (within the baths) for a cup of tea. By going into the canteen he had moved himself from the sphere of his employment.

But another lad, leaving the colliery premises at the end of his shift, was walking to the canteen for a cup of tea. The route he took was the normal permitted route out of the colliery. Before he reached the point where he would have turned off to the canteen, he fell and injured himself.

His claim was allowed.

A young girl was reaching across the machine she was working – taking a chocolate from a friend. The machine caught her sleeve and cut off her hand. Claim disallowed. It was not incidental to her work to have chocolate. But if she had been reaching for an oily rag ...

A colliery fitter was knocked up at 3 a.m. He was urgently needed at the pit. He got out of bed, got dressed, and in hurrying down the stairs he fell and broke a leg. Claim allowed. From the moment he was knocked up and told to come to work he was within the sphere of his employment. In the case of my own father's death evidence was covered up because the two witnesses had been "got at" by the management. Six months later, one of the witnesses hanged himself. Dad had walked past a wagon door which had collapsed, spilling ten tons of rocks and stones upon him. It had been reported as damaged, but the management had failed to have it repaired. This evidence was never revealed and my Dad's death was therefore ruled as "death by misadventure". Mum was robbed of her compensation.

Cases like these show how many pitfalls there are for anyone claiming benefits or compensation without the help of someone who is expert in dealing with accidents. They also show why workers should have union representation at their place of employment. The forces they are up against are not neutral. Vester and Cartwright in their book, "Industrial Injuries", say: "An accident means an unintended and unexpected occurrence which produces hurt or loss." They then go on to say, "A great part of the industrial accidents are the result of unforeseeable mishaps or untoward events which do not result from the breach of any statutory or other legal duty. The result is that in these cases there is no remedy at law for injured workers."

This load of bull is a good example of the kind of prejudicial thinking that underlies laws used to protect the privileges of industry and the employing class, who always prefer to allocate no blame and thus lay the cost of industrial injuries upon the employee. Although things have improved over the years, the onus of proving the cause of an accident still lies with the injured worker and the scales are still weighted in favour of the employer. The employer, generally speaking, never feels that it is his duty to establish the cause of an accident if he believes that might weigh against him in an action for damages. Far too often he will turn Nelson's blind eye upon the evidence and try to put the blame elsewhere. That's not how the Police work. When there is a traffic accident on the highway they belt along to the scene post-haste. Why? To get statements, examine the site and establish the cause. And somebody gets done! Accidents don't happen — they are caused!

# ON THE RAZZ

When I was working at North Gawber Colliery around a score of my mates developed the habit of taking a day off now and then and going right over the Pennines on the razz to a favourite pub in Oldham.[8] It supplied a good pint of bitter and some good entertainment. On the day I write about, it was Friday and we were on the afternoon shift. It was always on Friday when we were on "afters", which meant going down the pit at one o'clock until half past eight at night, that we opted for a day out instead of a day down below.

It was bright and sunny this Friday and it was always a pull – a real drag – having to go down the pit on a bright sunny day. So, about two or three times a year, we would bugger off to Oldham. The time was about half past noon and we were sat in the pit canteen, having a natter over a cup of tea before going into the baths and changing into our pit rags ready to go down the pit. Then one of the lads said, "Aw, bugger this, I don't feel like going down today." And another chap said, "No, I dunt feel like it either."

And the word cropped up, "Oldham", and somebody piped up, "How about sodding off to Oldham for the day?"

A motion was put: that we book a coach and sod off to Oldham. "Those in favour, please show." Out of the 20 fillers present, 18 hands went up in favour. So we 'phoned a coach to take us to Oldham. The other two lads decided to go home.

Tommy Hanson, who lived next door to me, promised to let Irene know where I had gone, and tell her that I would be home late. He went home, told his wife that the face was off because the fillers had gone off to Oldham and she went round to tell Irene.

Irene laughed: "I was thinking only the other day that it was quite a while since they had gone off for the day. Anyway, I won't have to cook his dinner tonight, because he'll not be home till one."

The coach arrived in ten minutes and off we went, waving a fond farewell to the pit, the lads eating their snap on the bus. We arrived at the pub by two o'clock, which gave us enough time to sink three or four pints before it closed at three.

At about twenty past we left the pub and went along to a variety club which had just opened. This gave us three hours to sink a few more jars and enjoy some entertainment. The club closed at six for an hour, so we left and trooped off to the public toilets for a wash and brush up for twopence.

Feeling a bit fresher we went into a cafe for a bite to eat and then, at seven, back to the pub to wind up the day. The landlord made up three tables so we could sit together. He also assigned two pretty young maidens to wait upon us, and later made some good hot beef sandwiches. The young maidens looked after us very well. They knew they would be getting a good tip later. When a collier has had a few jars there is no telling how generous he can be. We had lots of fun and laughter, and old Jerry, the one with the loudest voice, was a certainty to get up and give us a rendition of Granada, Begin the Beguine and the Spaniard Alphonso. Jerry was not a reight good singer, but he could belt it out, and was always popular.

But, however much we tried, we could never get the clock to stop. Half past ten arrived and Time! was called. The coach came back at 11 to pick us up and take us home. On our way to Oldham we had stopped at a fish and chip shop in Ashton under Lyne and ordered 18 fish and chip suppers for 11.45 p.m. We piled out there, dashed round to the toilets, then collected the fish and chips and ate them on the coach which moved off again. There was five minutes of silence as we munched. Then one of the lads, losing his cool because his mate had touched a raw spot during an argument they were having, peeled the skin off his fish and slapped it across the gob of his mate, saying "Shut it!"

His mate retaliated super quick by smacking the whole of his fish across t'other bloke's clock. And, before we knew it, there was fish and chips flying all over the coach. After a minute of flying fish and chips, somebody threw a punch. And then the inevitable happened. We were all amok, knocking the stuffing out of each other.

The coach driver sallied on regardless, knowing from experience that if any damage was done he would be well paid for it. Normally on these trips I suffered no more than a couple of bruises. But this time I copped for a lovely shiner. Billy Wild wasn't a big lad, but he packed a beautiful right hook. And I got in the way of it.

Then young Jimmy Wright somehow slipped, knocking his head on the side of one of the seats. He must have hit something hard, because it knocked him right out and down he went. That put a stop to all the jollying, so that we could see to young Jimmy. Thankfully he came round and said he was OK. Now we were all pals together again. For the next part of the journey we sang lustily, "I've got sixpence." Then gradually things went quiet, except for the odd bit of snoring.

Soon it was time for me to get off. The driver was taking each of us home to the door. I got off the coach shouting "Good neet, see you Monday!" and knocked on the door, knowing my dear little love would be waiting for me. She always did, bless her.

As I walked into the house, she saw my shiner, and exclaimed: "Oh my! What have you done? Come on, let me have a look at you love!"

I took off my jacket and, grinning at her, said: "Don't worry love, it looks a lot worse than it is." She sat me in my chair, saying "I'll make you a cup of tea. Then I'll look at that eye for you." Irene was very good at that. She would have made an excellent nurse. As I sipped my tea she bathed my eye and then put on a cold compress.

"Oh," I said, "I've bought you a present. It's in my jacket pocket." She got out the present and opened the box, to see a pair of gold earrings. They were a sort of diamond shape and studded with small red jewels. She loved them at once. Holding one up to her ear in front of the mirror, she said, "I'll wear these when you take me out tomorrow."

Then she turned to look at me, and burst out laughing, saying "You're a crazy bunch you lot. Why do you do it?"

"Well, its just a bit of fun," I said. "We've had a bloody good day out." Then holding my face, she asked tenderly, "Does it hurt much?"

"No, it's nowt really. I'll be OK in a day of two, and I'm taking you out tomorrow night, for sure."

Then, putting her arms around me, she said: "Come on, it's time you were getting off to bed. And you're getting nowt tonight either. You'll need your strength to get that eye better."

"Aye love." But I knew she would relent ...

# STEEL PROPS

I told you in an earlier story that timber for pit props sometimes ran short. Well, word got round one day that they were being withdrawn and replaced by steel props. I also learned that the steel props were stacked in the pit yard, waiting to be loaded into coal-tubs and sent down to the face. So, along with a couple of mates, we went across the yard to see what they were like. They were very heavy, came in standard lengths, and could not be shortened or lengthened to fit the varying heights of the face. Wooden props came in varying lengths and could be shortened with a saw if they were too long. These were made of thick steel tubing, with an inch thick disc of wood fitted at each end. These discs were put there to stop the steel prop from cutting into the floor or fracturing the roof. A brainless idea, if ever there was one.

We also consulted the lads at a nearby pit where they had tried them and the findings were not good. The props were heavy and cumbersome to use, and they did not warn the filler when there was a weight on by cracking or fracturing as wooden props did. They would either push into the floor or fracture the roof. Even more dangerously, they would sometimes "twang with a bang" and fly off at lightening speed, like a bullet. Nobody had suffered a serious injury from them yet, but there had been a few near misses. A hit could easily have smashed a body in two. It was because of these great dangers that men were refusing to use them. Many of the props were left in the gob – the entry to the coal face – and went missing. Then it was too costly to replace them.

Being concerned about all this, we went along to see the manager. We told him what we had learned, and we asked him if he was still going to send the steel props down. He accused us of exaggerating the problem and said the props were going down whatever we said.

"Well," I warned him, "You can send them down mate, but that doesn't mean we shall set them. Besides, we haven't agreed on a price yet."

"There won't be a price," the manager replied.

"There will mate. It'll mean extra work. They are heavy and awkward to use – and bloody dangerous."

The following Monday we were on afters –1 p.m. until 8.30 p.m. It was just before one o clock, and as I walked down to the shaft-head to go down the pit the fillers were standing around waiting for me. They were each holding a pair of steel wedges. They had been given them by the overman, who had instructed them to take them down the pit, saying they would be used to set the steel props. These wedges were 12 inch long and one inch wide. They were two inch thick at one end and tapered to a point at the other, and each pair was held together by a 12 inch chain.

While I was talking to the lads the overman came up and offered me a couple of the wedges.

"What's these for?" I asked.

"They are for setting the steel props."

"And how much are you paying us to carry them down?"

He laughed a bit and said "Nowt."

"Well you'd better get up to Burton" – that was the manager – "and tell him there'll be no wedges carried down without a payment." Then I turned to the lads: "Drop 'em," I said. And clang, bang, the wedges hit the floor.

The overman scurried up the pit yard to fetch the manager. He came rushing down, all hot and bothered.

"What's the matter, Joe?" He asked. "Why aren't you taking the wedges down?"

"It's extra weight, and if we take them down, we want paying."

Burton thought for a while. "Okay, I'll give you two bob a man."

"Three bob a man" I said. I knew I had him by the scruples.

"Half a dollar."

"Three bob, and there's no argument." Then I turned to the lads, "Come on, let's get down the pit."

"Okay then, three bob a man."

Turning to the lads again, I said, "Okay lads. We'll take them down. But we're not bloody using them."

On our next shift, we were told that the steel props had been taken down and were stacked in the tail gates. During the shift the props would be put on the face belt and each filler would take off 28 of them and lay them along his stint, ready for use as he filled off.

We had a hurried meeting in the pit bottom and agreed that the steel props would not be used. They would not be taken off the belt as they rode down the face, and would be allowed to fall into the coal tubs which would take them back out of the pit. And that is exactly what happened. The props were restacked in the pit yard where they stood for years, rusting.

# THE ROTA

Market men were a pool of standby workers who didn't have a regular job and were available to be sent wherever someone might be absent because of sickness or injury, or for any other reason. If there were no filling jobs or other face work available they would be sent to a day-wage job or to do repairs or other odd things which meant they were often paid a lower wage.

These men would wait in the pit bottom, near the box office, and the deputy needing one or more men to fill the places of those who were absent would ask the overman for the number he needed to man the face up. Most deputies would have their preference for particular men, choosing those who were less likely to be awkward about the stint they got or the working conditions. Or maybe they were more than generous with their chewing tobacco. Deputies were noted for cadging tobacco chews. Those fillers who were likely to be a bit militant would be kept waiting and pushed into bad or lower paid jobs. The overman – a sneaky weasel, always sucking up to the bosses – was the worst offender. He would go out of his way to stop some men from getting a decent job.

On this particular morning young Harding – a bit of a firebrand and one of my staunchest supporters, but in need of some guidance – told me that the overman was always picking on him and refusing to let him have a face job. One or two other lads had similar complaints. So I worked out in my mind that it was time we set up a rota system that would give the men themselves a say in manning the faces and allocating market jobs. I talked it over with the lads and decided to bring it up at the next branch meeting.

The custom for manning new faces was that when a face was worked out and a new one was started the men who were in the market would be given first choice to go on the new face. Market men would usually only man half a face, so the rest of the stints would be taken up by men chosen by the undermanager, advised by the overman. The overman's favourites were usually chosen first. But there were some, as we later discovered, who went from one face to another without ever having to do a turn in the market. These were the "lackey" types – plenty to say when the boss was not around, but nowt to say when he was; and always ready to scab when a strike was on.

Favouritism and victimisation had to be stopped. We decided that we would muster the lads to the next branch meeting, report what had been going on, and put a motion to the meeting instructing the branch officials to call an urgent pit meeting with the management and demand that a rota system be set up.

I explained how the rota system would work and how it would create a fair system of job allocation for the market men and the manning of face jobs. All future new faces would be manned first by those fillers in the market, and the remaining stints would be allocated by drawing men's names out of a cap. The names of those men who were not drawn out for a stint would then be put in the market. To make sure that every market man got a fair turn at the coal face, their names would be entered onto a list and men would be sent to a face job by rotation. The order in which names were placed on the list would be decided by drawing them from the cap, and this would then become a permanent list until a face was worked out and a new one had to be manned.

The branch officials of our Union were opposed to this idea. The President saw it as a diminution of his own powers, and tried to talk the lads out of it by saying that it wouldn't work and management would never accept it. However we pressed on. I had arranged for a few of the lads to speak and put forward their grievances to support the motion. I put the motion to the meeting and there was a chorus of seconders. It was carried. Two members of the committee and the four officials were against. It was also agreed that the branch would report back at a special meeting to be held in two weeks time. Normal branch meetings were held every four weeks, on a Sunday morning.

Word got around about what was happening and the management began to take an interest in the allocation of jobs for the market men. Young Harding got a face job next shift and the market jobs were shared out more fairly. The overman was hostile, resenting very much that his powers of victimisation were weakened. But that wasn't going to deter us. We had learned, by leakage, that the meeting between the management and the union had been a put up job. Neither side had any intention of supporting a rota system. They had also held the meeting on the quiet without inviting any of the lads to come.

As you may well guess, there was hell to pay at the special branch meeting. The President, shedding crocodile tears, pleaded that they had argued their very best but, try as they did, the management refused point blank to even discuss the matter. They regarded the rota as interference with their right to manage. "Bullshit!" was the immediate response from the men.

Responding to the President's pleadings, I explained that the management had the right to manage, but they did not have the right to victimise or favour one man against another. The men were the producers, and as producers they had rights too: the right to be treated fairly, and the right to have a say in the way work was organised. Good management should mean creative management. If managers were fair and took good care of the workers, they would take care of production. Managers should get around the pit and encourage men to talk and discuss problems. They should look into the work of their deputies and overmen. That way, they would know what was happening in the pit. They should not think of themselves as bosses. We knew, I said, that there had been some improvements in work sharing of late. But it would not last. Old habits would return, and that was why we must have the rota.

We had already held a meeting down the pit. Fifteen minutes walk from our face there was a waiting station where men used to sit and wait for the "paddy" – a little train that carried them out to the workings. It was at this point where we had our own pit meetings. We already knew that our demands for a rota had been rejected, and we decided to inform the branch meeting that we ourselves would begin the rota, starting on the next shift after the meeting. We also decided that on the Monday morning we would go down the pit, have our lamps tried, and then would sit down and stay there until the management agreed to the rota.

Come Monday morning my bus to work was late and I was doubly anxious to get down the pit as soon as possible. I rushed through the baths and when I got to the pit-head found that a lot of the lads had already gone down. The chair couldn't drop fast enough for me, but much to my relief the lads were standing around waiting for me at the pit bottom. The overman and the undermanager came raging at me. "What's wrong now?" they asked, fit to explode.

"You know what's wrong," I answered. "None of us are going to work. We are going to sit here, all day, all next week and longer, if that is what it takes for us to get the rota we need."

The undermanager and the overman ranted and raved, begged and pleaded, but the only response they got from the men, was to hear them singing lustily "Roll me over..."

The manager and group manager eventually came pedalling down and adopted the entente cordial approach, thinking that we might soften and go off to work. But pie crust promises were not acceptable. Then they tried getting tough, and soon realised that didn't work either.

"Look, get the men to work, Joe, and we'll discuss it at a meeting this afternoon."

My reply was, "I may be cabbage looking, but I'm not all that bloody green. We sit here until you have agreed to the rota."

Then they realised that time was getting on — it was past 8 a.m. — and that talking had to stop if they were not to lose a day's production, and more to follow. Backshift men, rippers, coal cutters and the rest would have no work, and they would all have to be paid. So the manager and group manager decided to give the rota a try and signed up to it. They also sent extra fillers onto the face, to be sure it was filled off by the shift team.

We still had to solve one problem. On 5's face there was a very rough stint, and very dangerous too. Because of the nature of the strata it was always in danger of collapse. For this reason there was no regular filler for this stint. It was always manned by the market men, sometimes with a spare man helping. It was agreed by the market men that they would take turns in manning the bad stint, strictly on a rota basis. Their names would be put on the list in order of the draw from the cap. It was also agreed that because of the nature and danger of the stint it would be shortened. To start the ball rolling I volunteered to be the first to work the stint although I had a regular stint on another face.

The rota worked well for a couple of weeks. The overman, much to his disdain, had the ignominious role of having to ask me for men to send to other jobs. In effect, the men had won the right to deploy men to jobs on a fair and equal basis. Then we had trouble. It was the turn of Arthur Roberts, one of my lieutenants, to go into the bad stint.

He turned to me, saying, "You're not sending me in, are you?"

"Yes, Arthur, it's your turn. Go in."

"I'm not going in."

"You'll go in or you will bugger off home."

"I'm your mate. You're not sending me in."

"I'm sending you in. It's your turn. You will go in or you will bugger off home."

Arthur then went to the undermanager, pleading, "Kenyon's told me to go home. He'll not let me go to another job."

"It's nothing to do with me", said the undermanager. "If Kenyon has told you to go home, there's nothing I can do about it. I'm not having a strike on my hands."

And Arthur went home.

On the next shift there was a repeat performance, and Arthur was packed off home again. Come the next shift after that, he still refused to take his turn in the bad stint.

Now I was really getting angry. "Arthur, you pillock. Are you bloody thick; or have you been put up to this? Can't you see, that if I favour you, we can say goodbye to the rota, and I'll be doing just what the management want me to do. It'll be back to the old system. If the men believe that you have been put up to this – and some of them are already thinking that – you'll be finished. And understand this: you will not work again until you do your turn in the stint."

Arthur saw the light, and did his turn. The rota was saved, and it worked. But my luck was running out. My health had been suffering because of the damage the dust was doing to my lungs. Every morning, around midshift, I had violent periods of sickness and coughing and became wet through with sweat. I had to keep having days off. Eventually I was sent to the hospital for X rays, and then strongly advised by the consultant to come out of the pit, or else...

Young Harding tried to supervise the rota when I left. But he had not yet won the full support of the men, and he lacked the skill and experience to do the job. Sabotage, organised by the management and their lackeys, soon brought the system down, and it was back to the old ways. Arthur was found a comfortable job in the airways.

## A DAY OFF

The alarm clock rang – woke me from my slumbers. It was half past four in the morning; time to get up and slog off to the pit. I dragged myself out of bed as usual, got quietly dressed so as not to disturb my lovely lady, and went downstairs to make myself a nice hot pot of tea and three slices of bread and dripping. Then I sat and mused for ten minutes until it was time to go off to work. Before going, like I always did, I went upstairs to give my Irene a good morning kiss. This morning she was awake, and as I kissed her, she put her arms around my neck and pulled me closer. I kissed her again. And again, and again. Then, somehow, I was undressed and back in bed. It was a lovely, lovely day off.

Three hours later, I awoke, feeling marvellous and at peace with the world. I looked at my lovely Irene, kissed her, then went downstairs to cook a delicious breakfast and brew some wonderful hot strong tea: carried them upstairs and, side by side in bed, we devoured the breakfast, talking and laughing as a couple should. And then we did it again.

What a pity more people don't take a day off! We did it regular.[9]

# III ROVING RADICAL

# THE NATIONAL UNEMPLOYED WORKERS' MOVEMENT

The National Unemployed Workers' Movement was set up in the mid
'thirties.[10] Sponsored by the Communist Party and organised by Wall
Hannington of the Amalgamated Engineering Union, it organised hunger
marches and demonstrations for the unemployed. It did tremendous work
but the official trade union and Labour Party movement refused to
acknowledge it because of its Communist affiliations.

I was not fully unemployed at the time but the pit was on a three-day
week, so I could join the small branch of the NUWM which was set up
in Royston, a pit village four miles from Barnsley. The village also had its
local unemployment office – the dole office – and the branch was based
on this office. Although we had only seven real activists, we had almost
every unemployed chap as a paying member. They paid their subs by
buying from the head office of the NUWM a small penny red stamp
which they stuck on their membership card.

On Wednesdays and Fridays, the signing-on days, we would stand outside
the dole office, collect subs and take up any complaints the men might
have. Many times when representing unemployed people during the 1970s,
'80s and early '90s, I have complained about the hostility we met from
some of the officials, but it was not half as bad as it was in the 1930s.
Then, the signing officers were not just hostile; some of them treated men
like scum. Many a time, after the style of the sergeant major, you would
hear them shout, "Put that cig out!" if a bloke was having a drag while
queuing to sign on.

The first time I represented anyone, it was a woman with three kids.
She had no money or food, and she had been to the dole office to see
if she could draw her husband's dole. They refused to pay her, and offered
her no advice about where she might be able to get some help. Her
husband had been collected by the bailiff and carted off to prison for 14
days because of a debt he couldn't pay. He had been picked up on the
Thursday, the day before he would have signed on and been paid. She
went to the dole office next day, but was sent packing and told bluntly

"There'll be no dole money while he is in jail."

The cupboard was bare, she had no food for the kids and no money to buy any – not even a penny to put in the gas for a light at night. Poor lass, she was at her wits' end. She went to see one of her local Councillors to ask if she could get any help from him but all she got was "Tha'd better go see the Assistance. See if they can help thi." "That's how much farting good he was," the poor woman said.

I knew of course that she could not claim any money from the dole office while her husband was in prison. The only way I could help her was to take her to the Assistance Board office and plead for them to give her something to buy food for herself and the kids. Here again, many applicants were humiliated and made ashamed for 'begging'. Mindless questions were put to them. The poor were not allowed to have pride in those days. Destitute, hungry for food, and asking for help to buy it, they would be subjected to an inquisition and then asked, "What do you want the money for?" What would you say? If you had any pride and spunk left, you'd biff them one. And sometimes that's just how it happened. People on 'assistance' were made to feel that they were the lowest, the least deserving, still with the smell of the workhouse on them. And it hasn't all gone away yet. Indeed, I reckon there are some politicians around who would like to bring all this back again. Anyway, I went along with this woman to the Assistance Board, and although we didn't get any money we did get a respectable food voucher to take to the local Co-op.

Another claim that I dealt with was when I agreed to represent a chap who had had his dole money stopped for six weeks. It turned out that he had been attending a Government Training Centre to learn painting and decorating, and had to live away from home there. He had volunteered to go to the centre, hoping it would help him get a job. After a few weeks his wife wrote and told him that they were setting on at the pit and if he came home he would get a job. He had also been promised a job at a local factory that was expanding. He wasn't all that keen on painting – indeed, he didn't seem all that good at it – and a job at the pit suited him better. He packed in the training and came home, believing he would get a job and earn a bit more money than he would as a painter. But he didn't get a job: the factory boss said "sorry" but they were not setting on just yet; and they had stopped setting on at the pit as well. He asked if he could go back to the training centre, but was refused. So the poor sod had to sign on at the dole, and was told, "No dole for six weeks."

We lodged an appeal for him, but in those days we didn't go to a Tribunal. It seemed that our social policy experts were a very sporting lot. When you appealed, you went to a Court of Referees, and thence to an Umpire. The court of referees, three of them, were more like goal keepers – crooked ones, guilty of more foul play, bad decisions and absolute obstruction than you could witness at a World Cup match. I did my best for him, but we had no chance. I was too green. I learned a valuable lesson though. I would never go to such a place again until I had learned to pull every bloody trick I could think of. When a decision has to depend upon the skills of the presenter and not the merits of the case, there is little chance of real justice; and less still when the adjudicators are prejudiced from the start, and their decisions have to take account of their paymaster.

Things did however begin to get better. The pits got back to full-time working; demand for coal seemed to be increasing, and there was the smell of preparation for war. Then, holy of holy's, in 1938, the miners were awarded a week's holiday with pay. That was fantastic. We were going to get a week's wages "for not working". Membership of the dole union had fallen off because men were getting jobs. There were only two of us left as activists: my mate Harry, a keen member of the Independent Labour Party, and me. Harry set himself up as a printer, and I put in more time with my studies at the Barnsley Mining and Technical College where I had enrolled to study coal mining.

# LEFT BOOK CLUB

The Left Book Club was founded in 1936 by Victor Gollancz, a teacher turned publisher. His idea was to provide a cheap and regular source of reading, "which would seek to inform and educate public opinion about the growing menace of the rise of fascism in Europe". It was no accident that the Club emerged within weeks of General Franco's arrival in Spain to launch a civil war against the legitimate government, which had declared itself Republican. The insurgents intended to destroy communism and create a fascist state in alliance with Italy and Germany, who provided guns, planes and troops to put down the workers and their organisations. It was clear that if the growing menace of fascism was not stopped, then war in Europe was inevitable if democratic freedom was to be preserved. The idea was simple; every month the Left Book Club would publish a 'Left Book' of the month. It would be selected by a committee made up of Gollancz, a publisher and socialist pacifist, Professor Harold Laski, an Executive member of the Labour Party, and John Strachey, then a fully committed Communist. In addition to the monthly book there was the monthly journal, "Left News", and "International Socialist Forum". The price of these was two shillings and sixpence, plus postage. Leaflets and pamphlets were enclosed along with the book and Left News.

The aim of the L.B.C. and the Left News Forum was to inform and educate the "non-politicals", and to create a body of informed opinion, a source of activists for the socialist cause, and to build up opposition to the rise of fascism in Italy, Spain and Germany.

The number of books, leaflets and pamphlets distributed ran into the millions, and they were read and discussed by people in the whole range of professions and occupations: middle class and working class, too numerous to mention. They were also aimed at people who had never developed the habit of regular book-reading or book-buying. The best and newest work on social, historical and scientific problems, written by left wing experts, was produced as material for practical political studies to help in the urgent struggle for world peace and against fascism by giving to all those willing to play a part in it the knowledge they would need. Within a matter of months membership reached more than 70,000, organised in about 700 branches and discussion groups around Britain, and many other branches abroad. It was a struggle I was happy to be involved in, but because of my limited experience, and lacking the skills of debate and persuasion, it was a hard, depressing job – trying to awaken interest among people who were more concerned about their own immediate problems. I would give out leaflets and sell the odd pamphlet, but without any real success. It was seen mostly as Communist propaganda, lies and inventions. Now and then I would get the odd bloke interested; he would listen but would never be convinced enough to become active. That was understandable because their reading was confined to the sports pages of the tabloid press. They were experts at studying the form of the horses and football teams, but most were totally uninterested in political affairs which, they felt, did not affect them immediately.

Even the official Labour Party and Trade Union Movement were hostile to the L.B.C., seeing it only as a front for the Communist party in pushing forward the demand for a Popular Front against the atrocities that were being committed in Spain and Germany. Things only changed as more convincing news began to emerge about the horrors of the death camps in Germany, about the torture of opponents to the Hitler regime, and about how Jews, Catholics, Protestants, socialists and trade union leaders were disappearing, never to be seen again.

My work for the Left Book Club was not very effective because, apart from Ernie Spooner, who introduced me to the Club, I knew only two other members in the Barnsley area. One chap, George, was a committed socialist, but long past his prime and suffering bad health because of a lifetime of graft and grind in the pit. He, like Ernie, was a reading man. Workmen who read books were never trusted by the bosses and, like Ernie, George had paid for that more than once in his working life. He had a good library of socialist and communist literature, and of philosophy too. Time spent with him was always uplifting.

The other chap, Harold, was at times a raving lunatic. He would rant on, parrot fashion, reciting stuff about the enemies of the workers: the monarchy, parliament, the military, the judges, the police, the law – the whole gamut of officialdom. Five minutes with him in that mood and you came away exhausted. He was a good man though, passionate about his socialism and generous to a fault, always ready to dip his hand into his pocket for any good cause. He was a member of the Independent Labour Party and would have no truck with the Labour Party. He believed that social justice would never be achieved through parliamentary democracy, but only through workers' control of the means of production and distribution. Parliament was an instrument for the maintenance and protection of capitalism – a 'gas factory' of capitalists, bourgeois intellectuals and working class pawns who had deserted their class.

I did manage to get to a number of discussions and meetings in Chesterfield, Huddersfield, Manchester and Eccles and to weekend schools held in High Flats, a large house high on the moors above Huddersfield. I could never afford to pay for residence at these schools, so the only way I could get to the lectures and discussions was by biking there on a Saturday, coming home in the evening, and biking back again for the Sunday morning session. It was at these schools that I met Professor Harold Laski, John Strachey and Konni Zilliacus. During the afternoons there were social activities and games like tennis, but these were not to my liking so I usually hopped it. The schools were of little value to me, the lectures were way above my head, and the speakers were on a different wavelength from mine. Lacking any common touch between us, I was mostly a passive listener, untrained in the skills of thoughtful reflection and note-taking. My interest in the schools eventually waned but I did pick up some valuable lessons on how not to present a talk, and also learned the value of the commanding 'one liner', delivering a vivid, lasting idea in plain simple language at the end of an argument.

As a rough collier lad among wine sipping chatterers, I felt the games of the gentry were silly, reflecting the ways in which they earned their living. In our rough lives of hard graft the games we played were rough and hard as well. One of our favourites was to go down to some derelict old coke ovens where we would collect stones and half bricks, and put them in separate piles along two lines, ten yards apart. We would then form two teams facing each other, and hurl stones at the opposing team. We called it the war game. It was good fun, but a bit bloody at times. We would also go up to the park to watch the clerical workers playing tennis, the girls in white skirts and the lads in white trousers, all neat, clean and well spoken, whereas we were rough young buggers. As a player 'served', the lads would shout "balls to you, love!" Tennis was regarded as a game for puffs. We might then go off to the butcher when he was killing, get a pig's or a beast's bladder, and use them to bash each others' brains out. Ignorant little sods, I suppose we were, but it was how the likes of us lived.

There were working people in Leeds, Huddersfield and the bigger towns who were doing something. But in Barnsley and the surrounding pit villages they were not much interested. A few of them would listen, and sometimes buy the odd pamphlet, but some were bloody rude. I was a lone rider without a horse. There was one bloke, a Labour councillor with a big belly, black suit, white shirt and black bow tie, after the style of Fred Elliot, the butcher in "Coronation Street", who would bellow out, "Ah see tha's been giving thi propaganda leaflets out again, young Kenyon. Tha wants to keep away from that lot. They'll do thi no good. Tha're a bright young man, an tha could get on, if tha learned to carry thi corn." Trouble was, I never could learn to carry mi corn. Still can't.

For its last six years I took no active part in the Left Book Club but I remained a member throughout its life, and read avidly every book from cover to cover. Their first editions still crowd my shelves.[11] But where was I to go? By this time the Yorkshire miners had affiliated to the National Council of Labour Colleges. Now this was an organisation that might suit my needs. Since few people today have heard of it I must explain where it came from.

# THE PLEBS LEAGUE

In 1908 a group of working class students who were attending Ruskin College, Oxford, were worried about the poor quality of the education they were getting. They tried to get it changed into something that would be of more use to them and the class they belonged to. Their protests were ignored so, like any workers worth their salt, they went on strike.

Their militancy was a natural extension of the struggles they had endured in their work places – the coal mines, the railways and the engineering industry where, at this time, industrial conflict was endemic. They were forward thinking lads who had picked up socialist ideas from their membership of the Social Democratic Federation, the Socialist Labour Party and the Independent Labour Party. They knew, from their own experience, that there had to be big changes in their industrial and social life, which was so dominated by those who owned the world in which they lived.

The Socialist Labour Party was most influential in developing socialist ideas through their cheap and regular pamphlets, written for working class people in a language they could understand. They published the Communist Manifesto, "Historical Materialism" and "Wages, Labour and Capital". They also organised classes for working people in which they studied Marxist theories.

All of this made a deep and lasting impression upon the Ruskin lads who became convinced that if they were to develop the class struggle effectively and throw off the chains of class bondage and wage slavery they would have to start by creating an independent working class education. The education they were getting at Oxford represented the interests of the ruling class and the capitalist economic system. It would equip them for promotion and lift them out of the working class. But that would be of no value to their work mates who, through their trade unions, were paying for this education.

Just as militant, forward-looking workers had, during the last years of the nineteenth century, formed their own collective bargaining associations

– the Trade Unions – their own distributive organisations – the Co-operative Societies – and their own political parties, so they would have to create a democratically controlled, independent, working class education. For education is power. It is always geared to protect and promote the interests of the social class controlling it.

The striking students organised, through the Plebs League, study groups and classes, so that socialist theories of Marx and the history of the struggles of industrial labour could be passed on. They also founded a journal, "Young Oxford", and the Ruskin Labour League. The Plebs League wanted to turn Ruskin College into a genuine Labour College, run by the workers for the workers. The idea for its name arose out of the studies some of the students had been making of the history of ancient Rome, and the struggles and sufferings of the Plebians who were part of the lower social orders. They saw in their own situation a parallel to the struggles between the Plebians and the Patricians – the bosses of the time. The League developed branches, and classes were started in South Wales, Lancashire, the West Riding of Yorkshire, the North East and Scotland.

The formation of the Labour Representation Committee in 1900, and then the disturbing election of 29 Labour MPs in 1906, had caused quite a tremor among the Oxford establishment. They realised that, before long, the Labour Movement would become a serious political force to be reckoned with. Summat had to be done, sharp. The leaders of the Labour Movement had to be provided with a safe education. Hence Ruskin College. The more radical students recruited by the College wanted to know how the exploitation they encountered in their working lives was caused, and how things could be changed. They got no satisfaction from their tutors because the tutors themselves were part of the establishment. They didn't have a clue anyway. Their environment and upbringing, their ideas, their language itself, were foreign to the lads they were teaching who felt that what they offered was only a kind of brain washing.

# FROM CENTRAL LABOUR COLLEGE TO A NATIONAL COUNCIL

After the strike most of the students refused to go back to Ruskin, and along with some of their supporters they decided to set up their own independent college. Becoming independent was a hard struggle. They were short of brass, and their only resource was their own energy and commitment. Despite hostility from some sections of the trade unions and the Labour movement, they firmly believed that eventually things would turn in their favour. They wanted their own independent, residential college and, along with it, local colleges to be organised around industrial areas where groups of workers met to study Marxist economics and Labour history. By 1909, the Central Labour College opened up and twenty students took up residence, most of them transferring from Ruskin. The first providers of financial support were the South Wales Miners, the railway and engineering unions, and other supporting local colleges. The courses provided were in English, Labour History, Industrial History, Logic, Economics, Sociology and Dialectical Materialism. By 1914 more than a thousand workers were attending local college classes, mostly organised by the Plebs League and the Central Labour College.

As the number of colleges and classes grew, the need for closer co-ordination increased. In October 1921, a conference of the Labour Colleges and the League was held in Birmingham. After a lot of argument it was agreed that a National Council of Labour Colleges should be set up. But full autonomy would remain with the local colleges. Their aims, agreed at the conference, were:

To provide working class education, from a working class point of view... through the medium of colleges, classes and public lectures – later extended to include free postal courses. To co-ordinate and extend Independent Working Class Education. To publish leaflets, pamphlets and syllabuses to help tutors and students.

From that day on, the NCLC was to develop, becoming the largest independent working class education system in the world. More than a hundred Trade Unions were affiliated on a national basis and hundreds more through regional and district branches. Co-op guilds, local Labour Parties and Trades Councils affiliated on a regional or local basis. All gained opportunities for weekly classes, day and weekend schools, summer schools and free postal courses covering more than 75 different subjects. It was in 1947, when the Yorkshire Miners affiliated to the NCLC, that I gained a real chance of a working class education, free of academic jargon – something that was practical and could be applied within the workplace – provided in my kind of language, easy to understand and to put into practice. It gave me the essential human link which the Left Book Club didn't offer – the common touch.

As affiliations to the NCLC grew, it was able to employ eighteen full-time tutor organisers in twelve divisions around the whole of the UK. Theirs was a beautiful job, and providing the organiser was dedicated to providing working class education regardless of the hours of work and he got results, he was king in his own domain. He had to organise classes, lectures and day schools around his region, and weekend schools where top ranking speakers came to talk on a wide range of economic and industrial subjects. Many day schools were arranged to bring people together to discuss urgent local issues and controversies.

Soon after the Yorkshire miners affiliated, the newly-appointed organiser visited me at home. He explained to me the aims and purposes of the NCLC. I was eager to learn and couldn't wait to get started. After some discussion I agreed to take a postal course on English. It was from this course that I learned how to write effective letters, reports from meetings, and, coupled with a course on wage bargaining, to draw up effective claims for a pay rise for the lads. My knowledge of English usage and grammar is still not as good as I would want it to be, but it doesn't bother me as long as what I write is easy to understand.

I then went on to complete 15 other courses, my favourites being heath and safety at work, claiming industrial injury benefits, claims for damages because of an accident at work, plus of course those on economics. The beauty of NCLC education was that, whatever course you studied, there was always an in-built bias to the socialist angle, instead of the capitalist bias you get in orthodox education. Later on, I became a college secretary – unpaid of course – and began to organise my own classes, discussions and debates. During my years of study, I carried out a number of surveys about pit life. These, I discovered, were avidly read by Coal Board officials at divisional and national level, but scorned by the right-wing NUM leadership.

Some of these surveys were about safety and working conditions. Because of my findings, I built up a good working relationship with the Yorkshire Division Coal Board Chairman, a good socialist, and I was able to get a number of grievances put right and to bring about some changes regarding safety. It was partly because of this that I won such loyalty from my work mates. But I wasn't popular with the NUM leadership. I wasn't bothered by that. I remember one Sunday morning, we were on strike and there was a mass meeting in the local workingmen's club. The Yorkshire secretary came down to talk some sense into the lads. But it was nonsense. He told lies and used subterfuge. I called his bluff. Later he told his Divisional Chairman "I had the meeting eating out of my hand until that grey-bearded bastard Kenyon interfered." Education and knowledge are powerful weapons. Because of my self training and the help of a practical education from the NCLC, I learned to hone mine to cut just where they hurt most. Mind you, I took a few bruises as well, but that's all part of the game.

At Christmas, 1959, the NCLC advertised for an organiser for the Yorkshire area. The previous organiser was leaving. I was tempted to apply for the job, but I was having such a good time at the pit, I decided to leave it. It was a hard decision, because the NCLC offered such a good chance of developing further independent working class education around Yorkshire.

But in January 1960 my chest got worse, and I could hardly stop coughing. Twice I burst my navel because of the violence of my coughing, and I had to wear a binder round my stomach. It got so that around mid-shift I was trembling, lathered in sweat because of heavy bouts of coughing, and had to throw up. The chap in the next stint to mine said he could set his watch by the time when I would start coughing. I was going to have to leave the pit, and this worried me because I could see the danger of my rota system breaking up.

In late February I ended up in hospital where the consultant showed me X-rays of my chest and explained to me what was happening. He said that although my chest was not at a critical stage, it was beginning to fibrate and if I were to continue working in the pit, I would only be able to work for five years – ten at the most. But if I left the industry there was nothing to stop me living a long life.

So that was it. I went home and told my dear wife what the consultant had said, and she at once replied "Well you're not going to the pit again, even if you never get another job." I told her about the NCLC job, wondering if there might still be a chance of getting it. "But it will be a low wage at the start" I added.

"Well a low wage is better than no wage" she said, giving me a hug.

So I went out and 'phoned them right away. They knew me because of the courses I had taken and my voluntary work with the NCLC. I asked if the job of organiser was still open, and they said they were now arranging a short list for interview, but in view of my work with the miners they would accept my application if I got it to them within 48 hours.

A week later I got a letter asking me to attend for an interview and oral and written tests. The tests would be held in the Transport and General Workers' office, and the interviews, later in the day, in Arthur Woodburn's room in the House of Commons. Woodburn was the President of the NCLC and also the Secretary of State for Scotland.

During the tests we had to write essays on Socialism, the theory of value, and take an English test and a few other items, plus an essay about the work of the NCLC. The tests were easy for me, because they were based upon written answers from NCLC Postal Courses which I had studied. The other lads, three from Ruskin and one from Fircroft College, didn't have a clue. You could say it was not a level playing field. They asked me how things were in Barnsley, and I saw they had cuttings from the Sheffield Telegraph, The Yorkshire Post and The Star about the activities of the Barnsley College in which I was involved as a volunteer.

In short, I was offered the job. They asked me when I could start. "Tomorrow," I said.

"Won't you have to give a week's notice?" I was asked.

"No," I replied. "The boss will be quite glad to see the back of me." I knew they must have known about my reputation at the pit, so I decided to make things plain from the start.

We had a discussion about work and I was told to go and take over the office in Leeds on Monday morning. I then left to get the train home to Barnsley. Next morning, Friday, I went down to the pit and walked into the managers' office. As I opened the door, I was greeted with a loud cheer and a cry of "Congratulations, congratulations, Joe!" coming from the pit manager, the group manager, and the President and Secretary of the NUM branch.

"How did you know I had got the job?" I asked.

"It's here in the Daily Herald," the manager exclaimed. "When do you start then?" he asked.

"Monday morning, I don't reckon you'll want a week's notice."

"Oh, no," the manager said: "Your cards and your wages are here waiting for you."

I was offered a drink, and I said: "Seeing as I am saying goodbye to you buggers, I'll have one with you." I did remind the manager that six months ago he had offered me £2,000 to find a fresh pit to work at, but, before I could finish, he grinned and said, "Bollocks!"

"Aye," I grinned back. "I thought tha'd say that."

And so I left, blowing my nose into my handkerchief – no more a collier. Such a sad and happy parting. I half expected them to break out and sing Auld Lang Syne.

## N.C.L.C. ORGANISER

Come Monday morning, I went to Leeds. The office was up in the garret of the Leeds Trades and Labour club. It was a shabby little room with a bare floor that needed a good scrub, a desk that had seen better days, a filing cabinet, an old 19th century typewriter, a duplicator that had been used to supply leaflets during the Boer war, two chairs and a long stool to sit about six people. I reckon this was a reflection of the previous organiser – a dedicated anarchist, and it showed – who had allowed the area to run down. There was also a sort of antique telephone receiver, which many a time I have wished I had brought out with me. I spent the best part of the first week just cleaning the place up. Irene offered to come and clean it for me, but I said, "No, I ain't stopping there all that long."

Within a couple of weeks I found a good reason for moving the whole caboodle over to my home, which became my office. I first saw the club secretary and asked if he had a more suitable room, but there wasn't, and he reminded me that the NCLC was getting the room rent free. I soon found out why. The following week the office was broken into three times, stuff I had left on the desk had been swept off and put on the floor, and the door lock was broken. When I saw the club secretary about this, his response was that I should not have locked the door. "And why not?" I asked.

"Because we let it out in the evenings for branch meetings."

"But I'm about to organise a couple of evening classes in the office. I've got a couple of voluntary tutors to take the classes and we are just about to send circulars out advertising them."

"I'm afraid you won't be able to do that," was the response I got.

"We'll see," I said, as I walked away.

That evening I decided to work late, and to occupy the office. Just after seven, five blokes walked in. Carpenters and Joiners Union, I think they were. I looked up and asked them what they wanted.

"It's our meeting night. We meet here every month to collect subs from the members."

"Well I'm afraid you can't have a meeting here tonight, this is my office, and I shall be using it every night."

After some argument, they decided to leave and see the club secretary. On reflection, I thought: this isn't going to do much good. I need to recruit these blokes, not alienate them, and I don't want to be sat here in this muck-hole every night. I then went down to the club bar, got myself a pint, and had a bit of a do with the secretary. I told him I would be moving out of the office next week.

Next day, I hired a van and a couple of strong lads. I went off to Leeds, hauled all the furniture out and brought it home. From then on, I worked from home. I 'phoned up my boss – old Millar – and told him what I had done. He was a bit peeved at first, but after I had filled him in with all the details he agreed with me.

Working at home was a bit strange – not having to rush out of a morning to go off to work – but I soon got used to it. In any case, most of my work was not at home; it was out in the field, looking up contacts, recruiting helpers and building up a list of students ready to attend classes. Luckily for me, I already had many good contacts because of my previous activities, and it wasn't long before I had a few chaps ready and willing to be voluntary tutors. The problem was to find students prepared to attend a class on a regular basis.

Central office was well organised to keep us up-to-date with lists of all branch officials of the various affiliated trade unions and other labour organisations, co-op guilds etc. They also provided lists of all postal course students in the area, especially the ones who had gained top marks. There were no classes running in the area I had taken over, but I did have a couple of classes attached to the Barnsley College. I also had been arranging with students from two or three NUM branches to start a class on collective bargaining. This was held in the NUM offices at Barnsley on a Saturday morning, and it turned out to be a very good one. The Branch Secretary of a West Yorkshire branch was eager to put in a wage claim for the fillers, and so we decided that the class would prepare the wage claim.

All of the lads, 19 of them, took on separate jobs to research wages, working conditions, length of stints, etc. Evidence from the best-paid pits and the worst was collated and a pay claim was drawn up and presented to the pit management. The pit was able to secure a good wage rise and an improvement of working conditions. We later learned from the Industrial Relations officer at Doncaster that instructions had been sent out to all the pits in the Division to be on the lookout for a similar wage claim.

As time went on and I gained more experience, I was able to develop classes, colleges and day schools throughout Yorkshire. Some colleges in Hull, York, Leeds, Bradford and other towns round about organised their own classes. A good day school, organised around a controversial economic or political issue, became a good source of recruitment for us. What a pity there are not the same opportunities today!

The beauty of my job was that I was able to push one of my pet subjects, health and safety at work, which led to the study of the causes of accidents at work, accident site observation, and working out claims for damages. I'll tell you the story of one of my classes.

# MR TUFF

At this time the Yorkshire Division of the National Coal Board were running a safety campaign to prevent accidents at work. They offered cash prizes for the best poster to bring home the message of the importance of accident prevention. I submitted a poster which the Coal Board said was very good, but they felt it was a bit too harsh and might offend. The poster was of a coffin with a wreath and the letters "R.I.P." on it, and below the coffin, in heavy black words, "He thought he could manage without timber. He couldn't."

I sent out a circular advertising a series of classes about Safety at Work. Bill Sales, the Chair of the Yorkshire Division and a good friend of mine, sent out details of these classes to all his pit managers. Instantly, one manager from a Barnsley pit, ever keen to jump on to the bandwagon, 'phoned me and asked if I would meet him in his office. He would like me to organise a safety at work class for his workers, and would pay all the expenses.

I went along to see him. His name was Mr Tuff, John Tuff, and all the men said "he is." During our meeting, Tuff said how keen he was to promote safety at work. Indeed, he took pride in the fact that his pit was almost 100 percent safe, and he offered to take me on a tour round the pit top, and challenged me to detect any breaches of regulations or unsafe practices. It was a challenge worth taking up, but I added a proviso. If I could find three or more serious breaches of safety regulations, or hazards likely to cause an accident, he would guarantee to pay for two pints a man for every man that attended the class. He snapped up the idea and we shook hands on it.

Then Tuff supplied me with a stick and helmet and we went on our tour. We first examined the ground level and watched wagons being shunted under the screens to be filled with coal. The screens are where elderly men or youths were employed to handpick stones and other pit muck from the coal being shaken down through a series of steel meshes that grade the coal and shoot it down into the wagons below.

We watched the wagons being shunted and then I noticed, twenty yards up the track, one of the shunters carrying a long steel bar. He was using it to lever over the points. I walked up to him and asked why he was using the iron bar.

"Because the fucking points aren't working," he exploded. "And we're sick of bloody well reporting them, but nobody takes any chuffing notice". Looking at Tuffy I said, "This is likely to produce a derailment and a hold-up in production".

"Don't worry," he said: "It'll be put right today."

We then went up the first gantry – the lower gantry where the coal was screened. We watched the men and youths working for a short while. Then I looked along a passageway that led to some wooden steps leading to the upper gantry. Along the passage there were big lumps of stone, discarded timbers and other debris that had been thrown from the screens. Turning to Tuff, I said: "Come on, we'll go along here." We walked about ten yards up the passage, and then I stopped. Turning to him, I asked:

"Have you noticed owt?"

"What do you mean?" he asked.

"Look at all this debris. The place is littered. You've got a hard steel floor here. Anybody coming along here, especially if they are carrying something, could easily trip over one of these obstacles and suffer a serious injury. It is not only a hazard, but also a breach of regulations, because you are obliged to keep and maintain a safe passage way at all times. Very bad housekeeping, what?"

We walked back to the screens and had another good look around, and then I noticed, by the side of the wall, three fire extinguishers and half a dozen fire buckets.

"How often do you examine these?" I asked.

"Every week," Tuff said.

"Don't look like it to me. There's at least six months' coal dust here. I'll bet it's two inch thick."

Tuff shouted to a chap: "Get thissen down here, and get summat to clean this lot off."

When the extinguishers and buckets were cleaned, I picked up an extinguisher and tried it. It worked all right, but the other two were empty. Then I examined the buckets. Three of them were supposed to be full of water but all they had in them was about half a ton of coal dust. The others were about a quarter full of fine sand covered by a thick layer of coal dust – a wonderful explosive mix if ever there was one. Slinging that on a fire could have caused a real old flashback.

Tuff's face was the colour of beetroot. "Somebody's getting a right fucking bollocking when I see 'em," he fumed.

"Come on, we'll go up to the next gantry," I said to Tuff. And I set off to walk back to the passageway leading to the steps up to the gantry.

"No need to walk back there," Tuff cried.

"Why?" I asked.

"We can go up the ladder."

I looked, but managed to say nowt. I had seen the ladder, and had it in mind to ask why it was there. It was the longest ladder I had ever seen, and must have been made for the job. It was anchored to the steel floor at the base, and the top was anchored to the fence on the top gantry. It stretched up and across a gap between the gantries.

Tuff took the lead, and when we got halfway up the ladder, I stopped. I looked down, and below, twenty feet or more, I saw empty wagons waiting to go under the screens.

I said to Tuff: "What happens if I slip and fall?"

"Tha'll not slip," said Tuff quite cheerfully. "The lads skip up and down here like bloody rabbits."

"Aye, and one of these days somebody's going to be 'rabbit pie'. Then what? You are the pit manager. You will have passed a stiff examination to get your papers. Part of that examination is about your responsibilities for safety. And here you are, condoning quite cheerfully a serious breach of safety regulations and putting your men at risk, which could easily result in a death. All for the sake of a thirty yard walk."

"Aye, aye," said Tuff, "I get the message, Joe. I'll have to take it down. But yon lads up there will scream blue murder, when I do."

Having to go up to the next gantry, we looked around for a couple of minutes. Here again were three fire extinguishers and six fire-buckets.

"No need to say owt," said Tuff. "I know what we are going to find." And we did.

Tuff, now a much wiser man, said: "I've got two foremen and a chief engineer. They all have to supply me with weekly reports about the service and maintenance of all the pit top. When I've finished this tour, I'm having them all up here, and won't I give them a bleeding roasting?"

We walked a little further round the gantry. There was a notice board on the wall, thick with coal dust. Tuff had it cleaned: it was about fire regulations. A couple of yards further on there was a door, also covered in coal dust. Tuff impatiently cleaned it himself this time. There was a warning notice: "Do not go through this door, roof unsafe." Poor old Tuff, he was as near to having a stroke as he'll ever be. And all this was before we'd even been down his pit.

He decided to call it a day. We went to his office, got cleaned up, and had a drink. Being a man of his word, Tuff affirmed that he would provide a couple of pints for every man attending the class.

The class was a twelve-lesson one; every Tuesday from seven p.m. to nine p.m. We arranged a ten-minute break around eight for the first pint to be brought in and the second one at nine. The class went like a bomb. Nineteen chaps attended, and others wanted to come but couldn't get there because they were on afters. Tuff enjoyed it as well. Together, we sorted out quite a few issues in a quiet way.

On the second week, 31 chaps attended; and they had a lot more to say. Tuff was a bit worried, but he settled down. Sixty-two pints weren't all that bad, plus a couple for me. But he also got a bit of stick this time. The lads were feeling more confident, and the tonsil varnish was doing its work as well.

On the third week, another ten chaps turned up. They had rushed out of the pit, anxious to get in on the act. Tuff reared up a bit at this, but agreed to pay for the eighty-two pints, plus my two. But at the end he said, "Sorry Joe, but I'll have to draw the line now. I'll pay for the pints promised, but I cannot afford any more after this week. The way things are going on, there'll be the whole fucking pit here before long". And so we agreed on eighty-four pints a session for the rest of the course.
And boy, did old Tuff cop it! The lads were in full cry. Old George, an ex ILP-er, let him have it good and plenty. "Tha allus on about safety, but yer never do out about it. The paddy in 4's drift has been working without signals for the past two weeks. Wires are darn, and t'only way we can signal the paddy to start and stop is by banging on the water pipes with an iron bar."

Then another chap had a go. "We're always complaining about the timber we are getting. We set three-foot props in the face, but most of the time the props we get are either two feet six or three foot six: either too bloody short or too bloody long. Short 'uns get slung, and we have to saw six inches off the long 'uns. And no extra pay for it".

"And that bloody winch rope on 5's level. It's had a knot in it now for more than a week. If it breaks again, and somebody gets hurt, yer'll be looking for blame."

Tuffy got busy scribbling notes down, and breaking out into a bit of a sweat.

"And while tha at it," somebody chirped up, "Shot firers are having to fire shots wi'art proper stemming." (Stemming should be clay, rammed down the hole on top of the explosive.) "They're using muck off o't floor or pieces of coal to stem up wi." And so it went on.

By the time the lads had done with him and downed their second pint, poor old Tuff was in shreds. He'd had enough. He thanked the lads, and then apologised to say that he wouldn't be able to attend further classes because of other work coming up. But he guaranteed that he would make arrangements for the club steward to provide the beer.

Then turning to me, he quietly said: "Thanks very much for setting this class up, Joe. It's been an eye-opener. But I don't think I could take another week of it. They've turned out to be a right set of bolshies. They wouldn't a dared to talk to me like that at the pit. Come to think of it, I've had a right bollocking tonight. If I come again, they'll fucking eat me. But don't worry. I'll keep my promise about the beer, Joe lad. When I make an agreement I stick to it."

Poor old Tuff. He had it rough. He was the first, and the last, pit manager to ask me to arrange a class on Safety at Work at his pit. But it showed what could be done by independent working class education.

## SAFE WORKING PRACTICES

Another type of class that always did well dealt with accident site observation. Here the lads learned how to examine an accident site, get statements from witnesses and prepare a claim for damages, the cardinal rule being: "The most effective way of making the boss more safety conscious is to make accidents more expensive for him."

One spin-off from these classes was that they became problem solving exercises for injured or sick workers who had lost their benefits because of the harsh judgements made by the government's insurance officials. And that led us on to a more general study of the whole range of welfare benefits.

It was equally important to make employees more safety conscious. Many accidents suffered by workers were due to their own disregard for safe working habits. I shall never forget one terrible example of this. My own neighbour, Jack, along with his mate Sam, was a 'shaftsman'. They worked regular nights, and it was their job to examine the winding rope, the heavy chains and couplings attached to the pit cage, the shaft walls, and the cross girders which held the guides that controlled the movement of the pit cage up and down the shaft.

The shaft at our pit was made of hardwood, six inches square, extending all the way down to the pit bottom. At each end was a pit cage. A steel clasp was attached, the open end of the clasp was fitted round the guide, and this prevented the cage from swinging on the rope as it was rushed up and down to the shaft.

To examine the shaft, Jack and Sam would stand on top of the cage, using a powerful spotlight to illuminate it. It was compulsory for the shaftsmen to wear strong leather safety straps which were attached to the cage. But Jack and Sam, being so familiar with the job, became contemptuous about wearing their safety belts. Their contempt for safety was made even worse because they had trainees with them, although they did insist upon the trainee wearing his safety belts. Lucky for him too, because while Jack was stretching out to examine the guide, he slipped.

To try and save himself he grabbed hold of Sam, who fell over, knocking the trainee over too. Because he was wearing his safety belts the trainee managed to stay on the cage. But Jack and Sam went over, hurtling 700 feet down the shaft.

Sam was battered to death as he bounced from girder to girder, on the way down. Jack's body was even more shattered – legs broken and arms and head missing. The trainee was in deep trauma for a long time and refused to go back to the pit.

This was a needless accident that killed two men, devastated a young life, and left two wives without husbands and their children without a dad. And no compensation. There were other accidents we examined, but this was the most dramatic. It served my purpose of driving home to the men that they had a duty to be fully safety conscious, not only for their own protection but to protect their wives and families who would also suffer if they were injured or killed

# POLITICAL ORGANISATION

During my first week on the job a chap walked into the office, no appointment or owt, but I didn't mind that; I was looking for work and anybody wanting to become involved with the NCLC was doubly welcome. This chap, Bill Hannaford of Wakefield, had just finished a postal course on Socialism, and was thinking about taking a course on public speaking. He wanted to become a voluntary tutor, but needed a bit more experience. He was keen to set up a class in the Kettlethorpe Estate where he lived and he wanted to organise a local Labour party there. Would I be able to help him with that? Although this part of Wakefield was Labour by inclination, they had to suffer three Conservative councillors because there was never any opposition. So Bill and I arranged a meeting in the local working men's club to sound out what interest there was in setting up a class and a local ward Labour party.

A well-attended meeting of men and women was held, all of them interested in setting up the party and a class. I agreed to write a couple of circulars for them to distribute to every household in the estate. Some of them were already members of the Labour party, but had not taken any active part; indeed they couldn't, because there was no local base for them to operate from.

We also developed a class covering Socialism and electioneering. Many of those coming to these meetings came for extra sessions on canvassing. Each member would knock on the door and put forward a case why people should join the Labour Party, and why they should vote Labour. I would act the part of an irate anti-Labour sod. It sharpened their wits and was good fun.

When the next local elections came round, Bill was nominated as a prospective Labour councillor and elected with a thumping majority. Eventually the ward finished up with three Labour councillors. Bill became a delegate to the Wakefield Trades Council and, along with a qualified mate, set up and tutored a class for Trades Council members. Then a Wakefield College was set up with Bill as secretary and the President of the Trades Council as chair.

By 1964 I had got the full measure of the job, and had built up enough contacts and potential tutors to plan for setting up a college in every town and township in Yorkshire. We were working to create politically educated men and women who understood the political and industrial issues that shaped their working and living conditions. The emblem of the NCLC was a purple badge with a question mark on it. I still wear it. I wanted more and more of the working class to be asking questions, questions, and yet more questions. A democracy can only work where the people understand the issues at stake, and have the knowledge and the freedom to interfere. But all this was not to be. The vision was destroyed by the very people who claimed to represent the working class.

# ENTER THE TRADE UNION CONGRESS

Jimmy Millar, the General Secretary of the NCLC, was way past his retirement age, but he hung on, anxious to secure the future of independent working class education. Although the NCLC was then at its busiest and most effective, he sought affiliation with the TUC, mistakenly believing that with the resources the TUC could provide working class education would become secure and develop even further. Millar also thought that a new secretary, lacking his skills and vital contacts, would not be able to withstand the growing pressure from right-wing leaders in the labour movement.

Alas, poor old Millar was conned. He was too honest a man to understand the two-faced character of men like Woodcock and Feather. Once he had signed away the affiliation funds of his Council he fell victim to a plot to kill off the NCLC. The last time I spoke to him he was a bitter and disillusioned man. The thought of a lifetime's work laid waste by the deception of so-called leaders of the working class movement almost destroyed him. Mind you, he had been warned in the past by people like Will Lawther, an old activist of the original Plebs League and a leading member of the Durham Miners' Union. His advice to Millar was to stay as far away from the TUC as possible.

At first, the TUC allowed the organisers to provide the kind of working class education they were used to. But in 1965 they reneged on promises made to Millar, and set about creating what I would call a training programme, as distinct from education. This training programme would make branch officials of trade unions more efficient as preservers of industrial peace.

I well remember Woodcock telling a meeting of organisers: "The responsibility for planning, organising and administration will rest with the TUC and control will rest with its General Council." Which meant that the students would no longer have a say in choosing the kind of education they wanted. He further added: "We cannot provide working class education after the fashion of the NCLC, nor can its purpose be to convert into active trade unionists, newly recruited or indifferent card holding members of trade unions."

Another quote of Woodcock's which has always stuck in my gullet came when I was an NUM student, attending a two weeks' course on trade unions. He said: "By what right should a union involve other unions in its troubles? It is up to each union to straighten out its own affairs, not to involve others. That is not the function and purpose of trade unionism." So what, I asked, does 'United we stand and divided we fall' now mean? I got no coherent reply.

So now union members were going to be trained. Trained in the way animals are trained to do silly tricks, or soldiers are trained to shoot and kill on command. Is it any wonder we are now plagued with something called "New Labour"? A middle class party pursuing a middle way, and the working class seen as an embarrassing appendage. A one nation, two societies party.

Evening and day schools were clobbered. Future training for trade unionists would be in the shape of day release courses, organised in conjunction with the TUC Education Officer, the Workers Educational Association, funded by Government funds, and by the local authorities and employers. We were no longer educators, but "officers": Ugh! Doing the very thing the Ruskin lads came out on strike against. It made me very unhappy and I felt betrayed.

Weekend schools were allowed, but the students' fees would henceforth be paid by the TUC. This sounds fine, but it meant that instead of committed students we got the professional student who saw a school as a weekend out. To make matters worse, the syllabus and the tutor were subject to TUC scrutiny. It wasn't long before I put myself on the slippery slope out of the TUC. Several times I was reprimanded for making my schools too political.

"We are not a political party," Vic Feather, then assistant general secretary of the TUC, sharply reminded me. "We are a trade union." Well if such a statement doesn't make you gasp, it did me. In early 1966, I had arranged three linked weekend schools to be tutored by Ernie Roberts, then Assistant General Secretary of the Amalgamated Engineering Union (AEU). I got a sharp letter back from the TUC refusing to finance the schools because they were too political and Ernie Roberts was persona non grata. Ernie was a well-known and greatly respected left wing union leader, but the TUC wanted no truck with him. Not having access to a photo-copier, I sent the original letter to Ernie and put him wise about what the TUC had said about him. I learned later that Ernie bounced round to Congress House and had it out with them. He was then accepted as a tutor but the schools had already been cancelled and I had no intention of organising any more.

I was severely reprimanded by Vic Feather for passing on confidential information. But I had been so angry that a respected and committed trade unionist was being blacked behind his back – I was having no part of it. I was in bother several times more. I had a well-attended class on Labour history every Sunday morning in the Miners Welfare Club. "Grimey" – Grimethorpe – was always a rich source of students and we never had less than seventy-five. On this particular Sunday we discussed the General Strike of 1926 and the miners' lock out. Naturally I had to be honest in my criticism of the failed leadership provided by the TUC. I explained to the lads that the TUC leadership was afraid of the strike, indeed didn't want it, and during a meeting they were having with Baldwin, the Tory Prime Minister, he just buggered off to bed and left them waiting. The strike wasn't called by the TUC. It was thrust on to them by Baldwin declaring that it had already started because the printers of the Daily Mail had refused to accept a scurrilous attack upon the unions. The Mail had declared that "the strike was a revolutionary movement intended to inflict suffering upon the great mass of innocent people in the community." The General Council of the TUC were forced to embark on a struggle which they really didn't want and were afraid of.

Well, it was only a few days later that I got a letter from Denis Winard, Secretary of the education department of the TUC, asking for an explanation of a report that had appeared in the Yorkshire Evening Post, about what I said about the TUC and the General Strike. I was also warned by Vic Feather that I was out of order in criticising the TUC. I was a TUC "officer" and was not allowed to criticise the TUC or any of its other officers.

The trouble was, I had never seen myself as an "officer". I hated the word anyway, and the last thing I wanted to be was an office wallah, arranging training courses, and not an educator.

So it looked as if Joe was on his way out. I had no further interest in the job. I knew that Woodcock and Feather wanted me out. They had a problem with the area. There were two organisers, and they only wanted one. I was the last in, and so obviously would be the first to be moved.

I was asked if I would work at Congress House, the TUC headquarters in London. Yuk! The thought repelled me. So I said, "No thank you". Then I was asked if I would take over Division 3 where the office was based in Ipswich, but again, I said "no". Then I was ordered to go to Newcastle and take over the area there.

I talked the matter over with Irene, my wife. She didn't want to move. She much preferred to stay where her family and friends were. I agreed with her. But I did warn her that I could be out of work for some time. "I'm not bothered about that, love," she said. "I don't think I could be happy in any of those places." So I 'phoned Vic Feather and gave him the message I had been itching to give him. I closed my remarks by saying to him: "We're never going to get on Vic, I've no interest in the job anymore, and so if you will give me six months' severance pay, a month's pay in lieu of notice, and a month's pay in lieu of my holidays, I'll get off your back."

Within a few days, I received my cards and a cheque for the amount I had asked for. The cheque arrived on July 27, my birthday, so Irene and I packed our bags and enjoyed a wonderful two-week holiday in Skeggy.[12]

# EQUITY

I was unemployed for the best part of a year, and then I landed a job as organiser for Equity, the actors' union, which also incorporated the Variety Artists Union. My job was to organise and recruit members employed as entertainers in clubs and pubs around the country. My office was in Manchester but there wasn't a lot of work for me to do there, so I decided to get out into the clubs where the artists were working.

Equity was a funny outfit to work for. It had a general council, split into two main factions. One lot wanted to recruit more members because the Union was short of brass and up to the neck in debt. The other lot were against recruiting more members because at any one time the biggest part of the membership were out of work, and to recruit more would allow more people into the profession and increase competition for work. That was a daft argument because the people being recruited were already in the profession anyway. If they were barred from membership it would make it much harder for them to find work in closed shops where Equity membership was essential. On top of that, a lot of the young artists breaking into the profession needed to be organised and protected from the lousy contracts some of the agents and clubs were forcing them to sign before they could get work.

Closed shops, which is what Equity sought to create, are fine in principle, but without democratic accountability to the members they can easily finish up by controlling the members. And so, after I had travelled around and got to know many artists, I worked out plans to organise a few branches based upon a geographical area. I started with the North East, and planned for branches to be set up in Newcastle, Sunderland, Middlesborough, Hull, West Yorkshire and South Yorkshire. These were areas of high activity in clubland, but completely unorganised. The first to be set up was in Barnsley. It soon developed into a thriving branch and started to ask some awkward questions. Some semblance of democracy was creeping into the union.

Although I liked the job, I didn't think much of some of the ruling council. I got on very well with Clive Morton and Jimmy Edwards. Charlie

Farrel pretended to be a friend of mine, but I could never trust him. Most of the rest got up my nose. One stuck up sod complained about my language. It wasn't posh enough, and was stained by my Yorkshire accent. Jimmy Edwards soon jumped on him about that. Then another mindless ape kept muttering that I wasn't "one of them". Later, over a drink, I asked Clive what the bloke meant when he kept saying I "wasn't one of them".

"You're not a Jew," Clive said.

"Not a Jew. What's that got to do with it?" And then I realised that I was about the only member sitting round the table that was not a Jew. During the whole of my lifetime I have never thought about people in terms of their religion or race, and this came as a shock to me. I worried about it for quite some time.

It wasn't very long before I learned of the consequences of the closed shop, and how much it can be abused. One afternoon in Manchester I was at a joint meeting of Equity and representatives of the Clubs Federation. We were negotiating grievances between a number of artists and clubs. One of the disputes was one that I had referred. It concerned a young woman who was in dispute with a club proprietor who had cancelled her act at an hour's notice because he was overbooked. She had been booked to play at this club for one performance at a fee of £80 at a benefits concert he had arranged. It wasn't until she arrived at the club that she was told she wasn't needed. But no compensation was offered to her. During the hearing the meeting was adjourned for lunch. After lunch Charlie Farrell, the leader of the negotiating team, announced that he had decided to withdraw the claim for my artiste. I learned later that Farrell had done a deal with the club proprietor: if in future he would employ only Equity members, the Union would let the case go by default. My blood boiled at this, and I later had it out with Farrell, telling him that I considered his action was the dirtiest trick a union rep could play on a member. I also made it clear that if in future an artist came to me with a problem my first move would be to settle the dispute my way – the way I had been trained.

During the next few weeks I settled a number of disputes on the spot, and with good results. I considered that an artist who was properly looked after would be the best recruiting agent I could employ. Then one Sunday afternoon an agent at Doncaster 'phoned me and asked if I could help him. He had a group of four young lads booked to appear at a large club in Barnby Dun for a fee of £4,000. The group had just received a 'phone call from the club, telling them not to come for their band call. Their contract was cancelled because he could not afford their fee.

"Okay," I said. "I'll see you in the club at eight o'clock." At eight I saw the agent who told me that the group had been given only five hours notice to terminate their contract, whereas the contract stipulated fourteen days on either side. No alternative work and no compensation had been offered.

"I've tried to see the proprietor, but he won't talk to me," said the agent.

I also learned that another group had been booked for a fee of £2,000. I read the contract, and it was clear enough that the club proprietor was in breach of contract. There could be no cancellation without fourteen clear days notice, by either side.

I then sent for the proprietor, showed him my Equity card and told him why I needed a meeting with him at once. He took me into his office and offered me a drink, which I declined. He was clearly a bit nervous, and at first tried to bluff his way out of it by pleading poverty because takings had fallen recently. He couldn't afford fees of £4,000 any more. I reminded him that he must have known that he could not afford high fees any more well before today. Why had he not tried to make some fresh arrangements with the group instead of waiting until the last minute, and so making it impossible for them to seek a fresh booking elsewhere? He sat silent. "You are clearly in breach of your contract," I said. "It is legally binding upon you to observe it, otherwise why bother with a contract? One way or another, these lads will have to be paid. You can pay them now, or we can take it to court and then you are likely to be faced with court costs too. My advice is, pay it now and that will be the end of the matter. If I have to take you to court it could mean that you will have difficulty in getting good artists in the future." And I reminded him that the other group he booked were also members of Equity. He paid up!

Shortly after, when I attended the next meeting of the Council, the question about the £4,000 I had recovered was raised. Naively, I assumed that I would get a medal for it. But no: I was told off about it, and warned never to do it again. I was not employed to settle disputes. They had a legal department for that. In future, any disputes that arose would have to be referred to the legal department. I leaned back in my chair, looked up at the ceiling, and counted to ten, and, by doing so, I managed not to explode. A week later I received a month's notice to terminate my employment.

A lot of the artists I knew were up in arms about this and raised a protest. Half way through my notice period, the Secretary of the variety section, and my immediate boss, said he was on my side. He 'phoned to tell me that my notice would be withdrawn, if I accepted three conditions.

1. I would spend more time in the office,
2. I would not visit clubs and settle disputes, and
3. All future disputes would be referred to the legal department.

"It's a bit of a tall order," I said, "But give me a couple of minutes to think it over, and I'll call you back."

I told Irene what had just been said to me and that my notice would be withdrawn if I accepted the three conditions. She laughed: "You know very well you can't promise that. I can't see you sitting in an office all day; and you know very well that the first call for help you get, you'll be off like a shot. You can't help it."

"Well, if I don't accept, it means the sack."

"You'll get the sack anyway. How are you going to be able to go into a club and not take a case up if an artist asks you? You know very well, you'll dive in and enjoy it."

"What shall I do then?"

"Tell 'em to stuff it, because I know that's what you're thinking." And so I called Reg back, and told him that I had talked it over with my wife and she had advised me "to tell you to stuff it. And that is what I am saying to you." So I was back on the dole.

I have to add that my Irene was not happy about me having this job. I spent too many hours away from home, and she was missing me. She was also worried because I was eating and drinking too much and putting on weight. Like me, she was more concerned about the family than about money and job prospects.

# CHRISTMAS

Every year, around four to five weeks before Christmas, Irene baked her Christmas cake. It was always wonderfully good and I couldn't wait to sink my teeth into it. Even when she was making it, I used to try and dip my finger into the mixture, just to sample the delicious taste of it. For my trouble, I got a sharp rap on the wrist. Irene always mixed the cake during the evening, so that she was never disturbed. She liked me to be there by her side to fetch and carry, open the packets and grease the baking tins etc. She always made herself look her prettiest, attractively made up, hair beautifully done, wearing a nice dress and the prettiest pinafore she had. It was such a pleasure to help her; watching her movements stirred up powerful vibes between us, and it made for such a rosy evening.

Irene never used a recipe, except what she carried in her head; never weighed things at two ounce o'this, or three ounce o'that. It wasn't her way. She knew by the feel of the ingredients just what was right, and just how much to use. Flour, sugar, currants, raisins, butter, spices and all the other magics a good Christmas cake needs – these she would assemble on the kitchen table, mixing bowl at the ready. Certain little rites of mixing and creaming the butter were performed; everything had to feel right, to be just right – perfection her aim. Gradually, all the ingredients, mixed to the correct proportions, were added into the bowl and then, when they were ready for the final stirring, Irene would pat me on the back, and give me a peck on the cheek, saying: "Come on love, you're good at stirring things up." Then she would hand me the wooden spoon and with a heart-melting smile would say: "Get stirring!"

Being a good stirrer, I went at it as hard as I could. It was hard work, but always worth the effort. I knew there was a treat in store for me. When Irene judged that the mixture was right, she would put it into the baking tins. There were three tins; a round one, and two loaf tins. The round cake was for decorating, and to be used at the Christmas party. One of the loaves was to be saved for after Christmas. The other one was for me to devour before Christmas. Plus, of course, a tasting bit which she always made for me. Before Irene put the cakes in the oven, she would make sure the back door was locked. She was a stickler about avoiding any sudden draughts or change of temperature in the kitchen. Then, with the cake safely in the oven, we would go into the living room. Irene would pour out a nice warming drink, and we would sit on the sofa for a minute or two, enjoy our drink and then, because the past hour had been such a luvvy, intimate one and everything so perfect, what else could we do? We made love. I reckon that is why the cake always tasted so wonderfully good and scrumptious. Love was its miracle ingredient.

Another wonderful thing about December was the gorgeous mince pies she baked for me, every weekend leading up to Christmas and the New Year. She would bake a couple o'dozen each weekend. It was such a pleasure and a delight to watch her magical hands mix the pastry, put the mince-meat into the bun tins, and then carefully put on the fancy-shaped tops before putting them in the oven. I must have lost a pint of fluid on such mouth-watering occasions, because of the treat I was going to enjoy. The pies were only minutes in the cooking. What a scrumptious, wonderful smell! I couldn't wait to get my fingers on one. But Irene would tap my hand saying "Wait, wait – you're like a wolf!" Then, laughing, "You can only have the broken ones." And she always managed to break two or three for me, so I could wolf them while they were hot.

Apart from those treats, she always baked fresh bread two or three times a week. There was no way she would have shop bread in the house. "Plastic muck," she called it. Only fresh baked bread was good enough for Joe. Indeed, one of the great pleasures I miss so much is that tantalising aroma of freshly baked bread, straight from the oven, as I walked into the house. Who could ever fall out with such a wonderful girl?

Every Sunday, throughout the year, there was a treat. After dinner, being stuffed up with roast beef and Yorkshire pudding, I would settle on the sofa to have a little snooze. Irene, wonderful Irene, would go into the kitchen to bake me a sponge cake, an apple pie, a few jam tarts and biscuits. It was hard to snooze because I could hear her singing sweetly as she baked. She had such a lovely singing voice, I couldn't help but fall in love with her all over again.

Mind you, I had to wash up afterwards, but it was a happy chore. What a lucky man I was, to have met and married Irene. She has given me so many happy memories that warm my heart – and leave a heaviness that can never be taken away.

# FAILURES

Self-indulgently perhaps, I find it easier to recall success than failure. But we had our failures too. Some of the lads, consumed by ambition and driven on by their wives, fell prey to the wiles of the system. There could be an easier and better life for them if they took advantage of opportunities that came their way. So they were sucked into the easy path of careerism.

First they went on day release courses at the university. That, in our area, was Leeds or Sheffield. Then on to Ruskin College where they were further softened. Then some of them moved on to their finishing schools as full-time University students. They were now ready to accept that frictions and antagonisms within industry were not the fault of harsh working conditions or the capitalist system, but the result of mischievous trouble makers and agitators. So, when they had absorbed their "EDUCA-SHUN!" they returned to industry as smoothly working parts of the system: as industrial relations officers, personnel managers, or Members of Parliament.

Several of my ex-mates did this. One hard lesson the workers soon learned was that the remoulded officers were much more difficult to bargain with. Because they had worked on the shop floor or at the coal face they knew all the tricks. Thus conventional education milks the brains of the working class and deprives them of potential leaders.

The failures, as I describe them, deluded themselves into believing they were still on the side of the workers. By seeking positions of power, they could be of greater help to the workers. But we all know it doesn't work like that. Let them really take the side of the workers and buck the interests of their bosses, and the boot is very soon planted.

Mind you, I nearly fell into it myself. Twice I was asked to be an industrial relations officer by the N.C.B., but I managed to resist. On one occasion they even visited my wife while I was at work and asked her to persuade me to accept the job. They promised a big house, garden, gardener and God knows what. She sulked for a couple of days before she told me about the visit – then saw things my way. Maybe I was a bit paranoid but I always saw offers of promotion as a way of divorcing me from the lads, and I didn't want that.

The policies of the TUC were another way of betraying the lads by taking away independent working class education and destroying it. The 'thinking' working man is feared not only by the boss at work but also by his union leaders. Henceforth it was to be, not education but training. A union of activists would not provide a comfortable life for the leadership. The lads would ask too many questions. Harder questions too. They would want to know Why? Activists must be taken out, re-processed and re-trained to become "responsible" branch officials, to work for industrial peace, to become "improvers" and "reformists", and to be impartial.

When Woodcock said, "It is not our job to turn card holding union members into political activists," the words burned into my mind, never to be forgotten. Another quote of his that always bothered me was when he said, in front of a class, "By what right should a union involve other unions in its troubles? It is up to each union to straighten out its own affairs, not involve others. That is not the function and purpose of trade unionism."

I know I have mentioned these quotes before, but I repeat them because of the lasting effect they had on my feelings about the TUC.

Some day all this will change. Technology has allowed the system to expand and survive. It will in the end destroy it. At the moment we are saddled with an effete system in which the rich get richer and the poor stay poor. But, just as progress in the past destroyed the feudal system, so one day it will surely rot the chains of capitalist wage slavery and its work ethic. If nature is forced to fight back we shall be compelled to think – to recognise that leisure may be more important than the kinds of work so many people have to do. Then we may rediscover what used to be Christian values – the conviction that there is more to life than just amassing material possessions. We shall learn to care, to think in terms of wealth sharing, to demand an end to exploitation and poverty.

NONE OF US CAN BE CONTENT TO LIVE IN A SOCIETY WHERE THE RICH GROW RICHER, WHILE THE POOR STAY POOR. IT IS NOT THE WAY TO HARMONY, NOT THE WAY TO PEACE.

## THE END

To tell the truth, none of it seems very important now. The things I recall most vividly are memories of Irene. Like when she would cuddle up to me during a long drive home at night. And the hundreds of little surprises we had for each other. There were many times when, on a Saturday afternoon, while I was having a bit of a drink in town with the lads or doing a bit of shopping for her, I would walk into a florist's shop, pick out a bouquet of red and white roses or carnations and pay the florist a bit extra to have them delivered so that she would have them before I got home. She would make surprises for me too; and love was always on our agenda.

Irene supported me passionately through all my troubles and fights. When we were on strike some of the men feared the wrath of their wives when the money stopped coming in. But not Joe; and if it happened that strikers' wives tried to rope me down, it was woe betide them if Irene got to know. She was my staunchest ally, my constant companion.

Two or three days before she was rushed in to hospital for that dreadful final visit, Irene was sat in her chair watching TV while I browsed through a book. I felt her eyes on me and looked up. She got up and, walking over, put her arms round me and kissed me.

"What was that for?" I asked teasingly.

"You are a good man Joe. A really good man. I love you, and I have always been glad that I married you."

# EDITOR'S POSTSCRIPT

Joe's and Irene's love for each other filled their daily lives, flowed out into the wider world to offer heart-warming friendship, compassion for suffering and anger at injustice, and made Joe a robust champion of the oppressed. Christian and Buddhist mystics have sought, through prayer and meditation, to attain this kind of holy passion, mixing love and rage. To Joe it seems to have come naturally.

His stories express this passion: poignant, enraging, funny or terrifying, but never just an entertainment, they pose moral questions – often disturbing questions – about the world we live in and what we should be making of it. I think he intended to bring them to some general conclusion. But, rather than guessing at his conclusions, he would have preferred us to draw our own. I offer mine in the hope that they will encourage others to reflect on theirs, and on the action we should each be taking.

Showing us the accidents and injustices, the humiliations and hardships, needlessly suffered by so many people in our wealthy country, Joe often used the short-hand symbols of his time to summarise the source of these evils. They were due to "capitalism", for which "socialism" was the solution. For a later generation, which has learnt that there are many kinds of capitalism, ranging from the Scandinavian to the Latin American, and that socialism, too, can mean many different things, these terms may seem unhelpful – archaic even. Rather than argue about their relevance for our own times, we would do better to focus on the practical realities with which Joe confronts us. They are simple and lasting, but often forgotten.

When in greatest need, poor people get most help from other poor people: women like Mrs. Nicholson, Joe's "God-given neighbour", and her cobbler husband; people like his Aunt Helen, Grandma K, and others glimpsed in these stories. But they cannot work miracles. What friends, families and neighbours can do for each other depends on their own resources and on the human relationships – the "social capital" – within their communities. If we are to prevent hardship and relieve poverty we must help whole communities in which many people are having a hard time by improving their opportunities for decent work, their earnings, their schools, housing and social benefits, their general stability, and everything that enables people to help each other more generously. The strengths of a community do not replace the need for wider social action, led by the state; they depend on it.

Policies which are aimed selectively at "those in the greatest need" – a favourite phrase of politicians and leader writers – tend to go wrong in practice, no matter how benign the intentions of those who devise them. Like Joe's corrupt teachers, distributing boots and toys intended for poor children, or the poor law and social security officials whose decisions he so often challenged, services selectively aimed at the poor tend to become poor services, inflicting humiliation and injustice.

Hardship and poverty may appear to be due to unemployment and sickness, but there are plenty of unemployed and sick people who live quite comfortably. It is powerlessness that is the fundamental cause of poverty – and its ultimate result. Joe's vivid portraits of the pompous inhumanity of the powerful – including Labour Party councillors and magistrates – and of the ways in which trade union officials can abuse the power conferred on them by a closed shop should remind us that power – its use and abuse – is what we have to keep our eye on.

The only services that poor people can confidently rely on are those which are also used by rich people. The only powerful people we can really trust are those who have to account regularly and personally to those who depend upon their decisions. At work, independent trade unions staffed by well-trained officials working closely with their members are the essential instrument for ensuring that kind of accountability.

Joe's stories repeatedly remind us that things get better for the most vulnerable people when unemployment falls to low levels and manual labour becomes scarce. That's when miners first got holidays with pay and, later, created the rota which ensured a fairer allocation of work. Full employment is important, not just as a means of avoiding a cruel waste of human talent and productive capacity: it shifts the whole balance of power at the lower end of the labour market, and brings about profound social and political changes.

These stories explain why a welfare state was needed – why, for example, we need good, subsidised housing to replace the slums which the market provided, housing which ensures that growing families will have decent homes when they most need them and have least income to spare for rent; and why the sale of such houses in areas like inner London, where good housing will always be scarce, was a crime.

Education is a central theme in Joe's stories. He reminds us that, even in the poorest families and neighbourhoods, all too often written off by teachers and colleges, there are able children and adults who have a thirst to learn. With wise encouragement and access to decent libraries – and now the internet – they are capable of educating themselves. When teachers – and particularly University teachers – meet students with this questioning thirst for learning they should try to help them to explore the questions they want to study, and recognise that in doing so the teacher may learn as much. They may be compelled to reformulate the questions to which they thought they knew the answers, and develop new ideas and different words for exploring them.

Perhaps Joe's most fundamental demand, running through all his stories in one way or another, is that all people should be treated with equal respect and should claim equal respect. He often used his mischievous wit to assert that claim. He and his family paid a heavy price for that robust independence. There were not many organisations that could long tolerate so free a spirit.

At the end of the day, what does such a life add up to? Joe was well aware that many of his neighbours regarded him as a failure: a bright lad who never learnt to "carry his corn", wasting all his book learning on a life of penniless social and political action. (It would have been harder for him today: he would have been swept into some New Deal "scheme". But so would Jesus Christ and his disciples.) Equally tiresome to him were progressive journalists who beat a pathway to his door, seeking quotes that would describe the hardships of long-term unemployment.

While Joe would doubtless have preferred to be paid for it, he was doing what he wanted to do. Secure in Irene's love, he would not have exchanged his life for that of the well-paid manager or administrator he could easily have become had he followed what he called "the easy path of careerism".

"This is a man," said the vicar speaking at his funeral, "whom we must commemorate, not with our words but with our actions."

# Notes

1.  Miners' strike: most of the coal pits were losing money in the 1920s. The owners sought to solve their problems in 1926 by increasing hours of work and cutting wages. When the miners rejected these terms, the owners, backed by the government, closed the pits. This miners' lock out led, within days to railwaymen, iron and steel workers, builders, electricians, printers and many other trade unionists coming out on strike. This became called the General Strike – the biggest in British history – but nine days later the Trades Union Congress lost heart and called off the strike, leaving a million miners to battle on against the lockout.
2.  Lift: top quality beef.
3.  Brattice Cloths: roofing felt, used to make the ventilation doors air-tight.
4.  Two foot, ine inches thick: this height meant the colliers had to crawl there on their knees.
5.  A weight started: the roof of the coal-shaft started to fall in.
6.  Stem the holes with explosives: fill the holes with explosives
7.  Woolley Dam now remains only as a name on the map and a memory among the dwindling generation who still recall it. The park was closed and the lake drained when the Coal Board extended a mine beneath it after the war. And now the mine is closed too, and it is planned to build a business park where the lake stood.
8.  Colliers' lives were very hard, and these sprees constituted a necessary safety valve to let off the resulting pressure.
9.  Each time Joe Kenyon took a day off in this way he lost a day's pay.
10. As the dust caught up with Joe Kenyon, it became clear to him that he would have to leave the pit. He was 45 years old. This third (and last) section, 'Roving Radical', consists of stories of what he now turned towards doing, drawing upon previous involvements, taken up before leaving the coal-mining industry.

11. Joe Kenyon had learned to mistrust the groups and institutions that shaped so much establishment socialist thinking and sought new directions for his energies.
12. Skeggy: the English east coast resort of Skegness.